WHATEVER THE COS

WHATEVER THE COST

ONE WOMAN'S BATTLE TO FIND PEACE WITH HER BODY

JENIFER BEAUDEAN

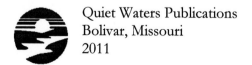

Quiet Waters Publications
Bolivar, Missouri
2011

For information contact:
Quiet Waters Publications
P.O. Box 34, Bolivar MO 65613-0034.
Email: QWP@usa.net.

For prices and order information visit:
http://www.quietwaterspub.com

Cover design by George Foster

ISBN 978-1-931475-51-8
Library of Congress Control Number: 2010943380

Author's Note

The story told in these pages is entirely my story and is written as I remember the events. The names and physical descriptions of the characters in this book have often been changed to protect their privacy, to include the depiction of some characters as a composite. In addition, dialogue and other small circumstances have been slightly altered to contribute to the flow and pace of the story.

Jenifer Beaudean

For
The mother
I love

The sister
I adore

The father
I miss every day

1

"New Cadet, get up against my wall!"
"You get up against my wall New Cadet!"
One voice. Then another.

The moment I was through the doorway, the tempo changed and the world sped from black and white to a blaze of color and activity. The first class cadets assigned to run and command Cadet Basic Training, or "Beast Barracks" were gathered like wolves at the door. Their voices filled the hallway, echoing back and forth, commands bouncing off the walls. The voices were rough and no-nonsense and the image of my mother and father waving goodbye in the hockey arena instantly disappeared.

"New Cadet,[1] get up against that wall. Line up behind your sorry classmates. Look straight ahead! Don't look at me! Look ahead. Stand up straight and look ahead. That's right. Look ahead. Your mommy and daddy can't help you now."

I looked straight ahead, not daring to take my eyes off the neck of the classmate in front of me. The din in the hallway was deafening. The sharp commands were bullets, staccato and fierce, strafing the long line of kids standing against the wall.

"New Cadet, what are you looking at? Did I tell you to look around?" another voice yelled. His voice seemed to shake the hallway.

Or perhaps I was simply shaking.

---

[1] During the first summer, cadets are referred to as "new cadets," an inference that the new initiates are not even worthy to be called "cadet." Once the new cadets complete Beast Barracks in mid August, they join the Corps as a fourth class cadet or "plebe."

"New Cadets, pick up your gear, pick up your gear New Cadets!"

We grabbed our bags and lifted them, still looking ahead. Mine was heavy and the framed photo of my family, tucked carefully inside, banged its corner against my leg.

"What are you looking at New Cadets?" yelled another voice, "Get down that hallway. Go, Go, Go, GO, GO!"

We scurried down the hall like little mice, each hoping not to be noticed or singled out, hot on the heels of the new cadet in front of us.

So it began.

I was ten years old the first time I laid eyes on a West Point cadet. It was the late 1970's, the time in which West Point admitted women. The decision to open the world's most prestigious military academy to female cadets was the subject of hot debate. Some members of the "Long Grey Line" fought vehemently against the change to a co-ed environment. Arguing that the effectiveness of the Army would be compromised, they railed that women would be a distraction to fighting men, that there would now be sex in foxholes. West Point graduates of centuries past were turning in their graves at the mere thought of a female contingent.

Amidst the heated exchange were valid concerns. Integrating women into a traditionally male environment, a training ground for the consummate soldier scholar, was no small task. How would their physical needs be attended to? How would discipline be maintained? Dear God, what if one of them got their period? But with the objections finally outvoted, overturned and otherwise squelched, the Army took its orders to make the integration a success. As women marched the Plain for the first time, the dissent among grads and many in the Corps itself lay in seething submission just below the surface. What those first female cadets must have endured as they broke the mold I cannot imagine. As a bright and precocious ten year old, all of this was a distant, faraway world of debate to which I was oblivious.

It had been a lovely day. Autumn at West Point is incredibly beautiful and on that day the sun was bright and the air crisp, the foliage made brighter by the grey of the granite buildings.

"You know Jenny, your dad took me here for our second date," my mother said. The football game was over and we were standing on the road next to Lusk Reservoir, right near the stadium, starting to make our way back down the hill toward the car. She told this story often. The words were all familiar.

"Aunt Barb made a picnic with enough fried chicken for ten people. I don't know how she ever thought we'd eat all that chicken," she mused, "but we sat on Trophy Point and had our lunch and I just knew that your dad was the *one.*"

I smiled. It is a wonderful thing when a child knows for sure that her parents truly love each other.

As we walked past the Field House, just ahead of us were two cadets walking at a brisk pace. I looked at their backs and the neat crease in their slacks, the way their jackets tapered at the center topped by the black collar. One of the cadets was a woman. She looked perfect - like a grand, fantastic paper-doll soldier. I watched her with amazement and wondered what her life was like. Her dress grey uniform was flawless, pressed and sharp.

She was also very thin.

She seemed ... amazing. To be a West Point cadet was clearly no small thing. To be a woman and a cadet, truly extraordinary.

"Wouldn't it be something if that was me one day," I thought.

And I reached for my father's hand.

Memories of that day and my first impression of the Corps were drowned in a sea of activities and studies. I was a typical girl growing up in an average American family. A committed and bright student, I was urged by my parents to study hard. By the age of fifteen I was painting masterful portraits and landscapes, had published my first poem, was achieving high marks in school and, frankly, wanted my own apartment. My life was an odd concoction of achievement balanced with a growing desire to build and make my own life. In the midst of it all, a rather unexpected seed was planted -- and in an unexpected way.

We were visiting relatives in St. Louis, my father and I, and I spent the week reading Tiger Beat magazine, which never in a million years would have been found in my home. My aunt and uncle also kept food in the pantry that in my house would have been considered contraband. Reveling in the freedom that typified those few days, I feasted on grilled cheese sandwiches made with Wonder bread, Chips Ahoy cookies and orange soda. My mother would have been horrified. Now, in a car with no air conditioning in the middle of July, my father and I were about to make the long drive back to New Jersey, where my diet would return to fruits and vegetables.

The cornfields flew by us as we chatted about amusing and unimportant things, and then my father made the single comment that would change my life.

"I noticed this morning that your pants look a little tight."

My father's voice suddenly seemed to fill the car. With my brow furrowed first in confusion, then in embarrassment, I looked at him and replied.

"Yes, they're a little small."

"I think if you could lose even five pounds, it would help. If you just cut back a little bit, your pants will fit a little bit better."

Now in fairness to my father, he only meant the best for me. He had struggled with his own weight all his life. With farm breakfasts of eggs cooked in bacon grease, my father's weight had always been a problem, even as a young boy. The pain of that reality, being heavy as a young kid, stayed with him. He remembered what it was like to be ridiculed, and I imagine he wished a different experience for his daughter.

Years passed and when my mother first met my father through the church where my father was a vicar, he weighed in at 240 pounds -- hefty for his five foot eleven frame. Despite his size, my mother fell in love with him and a year later they were married. With my father newly graduated from the seminary, they headed to Canada as missionaries to start a new church. Money wasn't just tight, it was nonexistent. Cutting portion size got much easier. It wasn't just the money, however, that precipitated my father's weight loss. My mother, who had an iron will, told him that if he ate only what she put in front of him, he'd lose weight. Sure enough, sixty-five pounds later, my father looked and felt terrific. To his credit, and my mother's, he kept the weight off for the rest of his life.

There was a history, therefore, in my father's comment to me in the car that late afternoon in July. He meant well. He couldn't possibly have suspected the instantaneous transformation that would take place in my perception of myself. It had never occurred to me that my shape and size wasn't acceptable.

And I was not heavy. I was an average, healthy young girl.

Had my father been able to see the course of events a simple comment would cause, he would have burned his own hands rather than lay the groundwork for the set of repercussions that would follow.

But he didn't.

As with so many adults in a culture where thinness is celebrated, he had no idea that a single word would put wheels in motion that I would feel for decades. With no concept of the enormous turn of events that had just occurred in his daughter's life, he changed the subject to fishing and watched the road. Where I was sitting, however, the world had just flipped on its head. I resolved to eat less and wondered at the sudden loss of my father's approval. What would become an ever-present battle with my waistline began to follow me through my every day and for years to come.

It was now a primary focus even on R Day.[2]

I followed my classmates as we practically pushed each other down the stairs in our hurry to get out of the hockey arena and onto the waiting buses. The firsties were already aboard, lying in wait.

"All the way to the back, all the way to the back!" one yelled, "Fill every seat New Cadets!"

Every seat filled, maximum efficiency. This is the Army way, a way that I knew shockingly little about, but was soon to learn intimately.

We all changed into a hideous uniform -- black athletic shorts and a white t-shirt with black trim and an image of the Academy crest. Shirt tucked in, no sloppiness permitted. We sported black socks pulled up to the knees finished by black low quarters. Finally, a series of mysterious tags hung by strings and a safety pin from our shorts.

The machinery that is West Point was thoroughly ready for the arrival, in-processing and training of fourteen hundred new cadets. This cadre, and every group of cadet leaders before them, was completely prepared. For several weeks prior to our arrival they had practiced the process and movement of the new cadets through each in-processing station. R Day moved like clockwork, just as it had for decades.

Each "station" had a specific purpose. There was a saluting station, where we learned to salute. There was another where we learned to execute certain military marching movements and another for the proper wear of our uniform. There were drink stations along the way so that we didn't get dehydrated. There were papers where we signed our lives away. At every station, every issue point, every rite of passage during that day, an upper class cadet made a simple mark on one of the tags pinned to our shorts. Each cadet was a cog in a massive wheel, and over the hours, I became a cog.

---

[2] "R Day," or Report Day, is the first day for an incoming class of new cadets.

"Follow the green tape to the next station New Cadet," an upperclassman said tersely. Spotting the green tape stuck to the concrete, off I went, scurrying down the tape to some unknown destination. If I had dared to look up from where my eyes focused straight ahead, I would have seen the meticulous order of it all, the new cadets following colored tapes along the ground, moving systematically from station to station, trotting along like terrified, disoriented mice in an endless maze.

It was a different planet, a different world.

And I knew I was in for the fight of my life.

2

Fall 1986.

"Okay now, try and put your whole body into it," my father called from across the yard.

"Okay," I called back enthusiastically and, from a kneeling position, threw the cursed basketball with all my might.

All in preparation for the PAE, or Physical Aptitude Examination, required for admittance to West Point.

The Road to R Day was long and involved. I sometimes wondered if the sheer number of steps and details associated with applying helped eliminate those who might not want cadet life badly enough. High SAT scores and good grades were just the beginning of the long list of admission requirements. There was a thorough medical exam. Admission to the Academy required a congressional nomination, which had its own application and interview process. There was another interview with the West Point committee itself, and then finally, the PAE -- a physical fitness test that included standing long jump, shuttle run, flexed arm hang for women, pull-ups for men, and basketball throw from a kneeling position.

My father and I stood in our backyard on many an evening to practice the basketball throw. I was not terribly coordinated, nor, at this point in my life, did I have a great deal of upper body strength. Regardless, with all my might I would heave the ball toward my father, who would mark the spot. Then we would measure carefully, stretching the tape out to the mark, examining it together to evaluate my progress.

Sometimes, the news was good.

Sometimes, not so good.

But I was determined.

I made the decision to apply to West Point with a shocking lack of forethought. After my first glimpse of the Academy as a young girl, I had largely set aside any thoughts about becoming a cadet. One day at school, however, passing a window with college brochures, I saw a photo of a West Point cadet. All the feelings of that childhood day, nearly ten years earlier, came rushing back. With little real contemplation and almost entirely at that very moment, I made the decision that West Point was to be my future. From that instant I threw my whole heart, my entire being, all of my diehard commitment and gusto, into gaining admission to the United States Military Academy.

My reasons for applying were mixed. The Military Academy was an exceptional school -- challenging, unique, with a fabulous reputation. Even at eighteen, I knew that if I could graduate from this school, not just any college, but *this* school, this impossible West Point, I could write my ticket. In a family where money was tight, this was my opportunity to create an amazing foundation for my life.[3] Instinctively, I saw that West Point could be a starting point for the incredible career and the life of adventure that I had always envisioned. And I loved my country -- "my America," as I often called it -- and believed it was honorable to serve.

I felt that if I could do this, I could do *anything*. With everything I had, I staked my future and in a sense, my very life, on West Point.

As the fall of my senior year in high school came to a close, the pieces were nearly all in place. I threw the miserable basketball and passed the Physical Aptitude Exam, won the nomination from Congresswoman Marge Roukema of New Jersey, scored well enough on the SAT, did community service candy striping at the local hospital, lead clubs and taught

---

[3] Cadets do not pay for their education at West Point. Instead, they are obligated to serve in the military after graduation.

Sunday School and was selected to co-captain the women's cross country team. All of it added up to admission to West Point.

The acceptance letter arrived on my mother's birthday in early December. She was stirring a pot on the stove as she handed me the white envelope. I looked at it, terrified. I carefully opened the flap, pulled the letter out and skimmed the words quickly to get to the bottom line. I was granted admission to the Academy and was invited to report between "0800 and 1000 hours" on July 1, 1987.[4] My mother's face reflected her mixed happiness and doubt. My father glowed with pride. Dinner cooked on the stove and the aroma of spaghetti sauce and garlic filled the house, but I was oblivious, staring at the official letter I held carefully in my hands, reading it again and again. I looked at my mother.

"I got in," I said, and wept with relief.

The morning of R Day I lay in my bed, my eyes just open. The white curtains on the windows in my bedroom, all cheerful with their eyelet ruffles, were still. Not a breath of air moved them and I knew it would be hot later in the day. I looked up at the enormous crack in the ceiling and felt my back and bottom, my arms and shoulders sinking into the bed, the bed my father built with hand tools in the days when they could barely afford food, no less furniture. Days marked by a cold house in the winter and in the summer, salads of dandelion greens that my mother literally picked in the front yard. Money was tight. But now I could pay my own way and *make* my own way.

My overnight bag sat on the floor next to the closet, filled with, as instructed by the Academy, twenty pairs of plain white panties, ten white bras, toiletries -- and one photo, which I had carefully arranged with a collage of my family. There was little else in the bag. The Academy had been very specific. West Point would now run and supply my entire life.

---

[4] July 1, 1987 was Report Day, or "R Day" for the class of 1991.

All of my uniforms would be cadet issue and plebes[5] were not allowed to wear civilian clothes.

I wiggled my toes under the covers, feeling cozy and safe for one last second.

My father appeared at the door.

"C'mon," he said, "we should get going." He was trying to be brave. I could see the sadness in his face, around his eyes. I adored him.

The pain of leaving warred with the excitement of a new life ahead. Obediently, I threw my legs over the side of the bed and put my feet on the worn rug. I looked in the mirror at my hair, frizzy and off-color from the home perm I had given myself two days before. It seemed like a good idea at the time. Less fuss, less muss while engaged in military training at all hours of the day and night for the next six weeks.

I looked ridiculous.

I should have just shaved my head and been done with it.

But as I walked to the scale in my parents' bedroom, I had bigger fish to fry. To get through R Day, I needed to make weight.

Padding across the hardwood floor in my bare feet, I pulled the scale out of my mother's closet. With trepidation I put it on the most level part of the floor, positioning it carefully, as if this would somehow magically make a difference, stepped on the scale and watched the dial climb up past 100 pounds. According to the scale I weighed 134 pounds. I was never sure just how accurate the old, worn-out scale was, but I was at the low end of my weight range. With a height of barely 5'4", medium bone structure and ample breasts, I was simply not meant to be skinny. Much to my chagrin and frustration, I would never look like the tall, lanky models strutting Chanel in the fashion magazines I so enjoyed. They were long-legged and they made Galliano and Ralph Lauren look sharp, crisp

---

[5] First year cadets are referred to as fourth class cadets, or plebes. Slang terms also include beanhead or smack.

and impeccable. The most I could ever hope for was a healthy, compact body with a strong set of muscles. My mother claimed I had a "healthy glow." My mother's best friend had once commented that I would likely live a long life, as I was so "sturdy."

"Sturdy?" I thought with sarcasm, visualizing the models in my favorite fashion magazines, with their tiny waists and towering forms, "well that's just terrific."

Now, after a month and a half of near starvation, I weighed my lowest since the sixth grade. I could now wear pants that had fit me as a "sturdy" twelve year old. Truth be told, the pressure to be thin came from all sides. Mr. Richards, my cross country coach, encouraged me to lose ten pounds when I captained the girls cross country team.

"Jen, if you could take off ten pounds you'd lead the pack," he said.

His comments only reinforced the continuous feedback that suggested that I was too large, not acceptable as I was. That I charged up the hills during the races, passing the less determined, was less important than size. No matter the source, there seemed to be an ever underlying implication that, while I was a gifted, creative, articulate young woman, I would be better if I were thinner.

The next layer of pressure was the desire to lose weight for prom season. If only I could be a bit smaller I could fit into just the right dress. My father once again took an active role in my quest for the "right size," and drew a cartoon of me standing triumphant on a scale that measured 134 pounds with a little road that was marked "Prom" and "West Point."

As if all of this size and weight pressure were not enough, my father's family was practically the "weight police." The focus on size and shape was continuous. A visit that spring to the family matriarch, Aunt Birdie, began with a person by person rundown of who was fat and who was not, even before I made it through the front door.

"Wellllll," Aunt Birdie would start with her thick Midwestern lilt, "Betty Mason sure has gotten heeeavy. She really just can't seem to trim down. And Uncle Denny, well he's just had a heck of a time losing that ten pounds since he had the gout last spring." Interestingly, all of this "thin and not thin" dialogue took place over heavy meals of pot roast, biscuits, mashed potatoes and a hefty slice of blackberry pie with homemade ice cream.

I was fourteen when Aunt Birdie looked at me from across the Dutch oven and big wooden spoon.

"Now aren't you a cute, round young woman Jenifer."

Round? I wanted to poke her eye out.

Now the stakes were higher. The United States Military Academy was a no-nonsense sort of place. The literature made it clear that there would be a weigh-in on the first day and it would behoove young would-be cadets to get their asses thin and within the weight limit. I looked down at the scale. By some miracle, my weight appeared to be right around the requirement, which was 134 pounds for a 5'4" frame. Of course, that was assuming that the old, beat-up scale was correct. In a few hours I would step on the scale at West Point, which was no doubt less than twenty years old and undoubtedly more accurate. I could only hope that I would be thin enough.

So much was riding on this day.

I walked into the kitchen. I had been hungry for days, beating my body into submission, trying to stay at a weight that it clearly didn't want to keep. The battle was relentless. It was as if I could glance at a blueberry muffin and gain a pound. And I loved food. Early on I understood the wonderful experiences that life can offer and the fact that wonderful foods are a part of that experience. I loved to eat and my relationship with food had become emotional as well as physical. Even with West Point just hours away, I was fantasizing about Belgian waffles, how warm and comforting they would feel, especially with my nerves standing on end. Belgian waffles, preferably with real maple syrup, not the fake crap ... and plenty of butter.

As I appeared at the doorway, my mother looked at me from the stove, where she had made breakfast every morning of my life. The irony was not lost on me. My mother was a lifelong pacifist and couldn't imagine anything more ridiculous than her daughter attending a military academy to learn how to be a soldier. In her opinion, if women ran the world, war would be a thing of the past. But this was my dream, and loving mothers help their children chase their dreams. My entire family had been a part of my weight loss crusade over the last eight weeks. In keeping with the familial commitment to my success, she put a soft boiled egg in a little eggcup on the table in front of me.

She didn't say what she was thinking, but I knew her thoughts. She wished that even at this late date I would change my mind. We had always struggled in our relationship, her determination to raise a decent human being battling with my fierce sense of independence. We fought constantly. We also loved each other intensely, finished each other's sentences, knew each others thoughts. The truth was that we were markedly alike. I knew that she already hated West Point, hated that we lived in a world that required a standing Army, hated my new commitment to that Army -- and thought this entire scenario was completely absurd.

As my father began the breakfast prayer, I looked sadly at the little egg in the dish in front of me. Here I was on one of the most important days in my life and I would have to go hungry, save this sorry little egg.

We bowed our heads.

"Lord, we pray for Jenifer today ..." my father started.

But I was praying my own prayer.

"Lord, if you could help me pass this fucking weigh-in this morning, I'd really appreciate it," I prayed silently. My view of God was a little more flexible than my father's. And besides, in the weight category, I needed all the help I could get.

3

The United States Military Academy sits on a point jutting out of the west bank of the Hudson River, about an hour north of New York City. At one of the River's narrowest points, George Washington saw that West Point had strategic value, and ordered military strongholds built there during the Revolutionary War to control river traffic. As the fight for independence progressed, he located his military headquarters at West Point and ordered a great iron chain weighing 150 tons be stretched across the Hudson to keep the British from making their way upstream. West Point was never lost during the Revolutionary War and came to symbolize the country's resilience and bright future. In 1802, Thomas Jefferson turned the fortification into a military academy. West Point became one of the country's first engineering schools. In the 1800's, graduates built roads, canals and bridges. They explored the territory west of the Mississippi River and fought the nation's wars. Both sides during the Civil War were led by officers educated at West Point. Graduates of the Academy distinguished themselves in nearly every walk of life and included Ulysses S. Grant, Robert E. Lee, Dwight Eisenhower, Douglas MacArthur and astronaut Buzz Aldrin.

West Point is physically majestic, solemn, beautiful ... and intimidating. Nearly the entire cadet area is constructed of granite, which reflects the stalwartness of the military tradition entrenched there. There is an extensive library and academic buildings for the study of nearly every discipline. Cadets live in the barracks and spend the bulk of their time struggling through academic classes and military training during their four years. Cadets must begin and end with their class. There are no college transfers. Cadets cannot be married and must be under the age of twenty two when they report. The cadet experience is meant to be focused and driven.

And nearly a third drop out along the way.

Thousands of tourists are awed each year, looking at cadet life from a distance, looking at fish from a safe, dry distance outside the fishbowl. They stare at the Academy from the edge of the massive grassy Plain that lies like a flawless green carpet in front of Washington Hall. As they look at the statue of George Washington on his horse guarding the entrance of the cadet area, most have no idea of the scope of the challenge that each cadet will face in order to graduate. And no awe is greater than that of the new cadet, braving the unknown to become one of the proud.

By the middle of R Day, I was completely miserable. It wasn't even noon yet, but my arms were tired from the weight of the duffel bag I was carting around and the heat of the sun blistered my already home-perm-scorched head. Between the grumble of my stomach, the burn of my scalp, excitement, palpable anxiety over my weight and a sense of impending homesickness, I hardly knew what to think about first.

I had deliberated about what to wear. What did a reader of *Vogue*, a young woman dying to be a great leader and, simultaneously, Audrey Hepburn wear to R-Day at West Point? The welcome packet from the Academy had suggested purchasing low quarter shoes ahead of time, or, alternately, dying a pair of loafers black. With the family budget tight, I had taken the latter route. My little loafers looked sadly and obviously dyed.

My leg hurt from my bag banging against it as I pinged[6] from station to station. I was overwhelmed with the enormity of things to learn and by the yelling and hazing that accompanied them. Passing a mirror, I saw my reflection and felt an

---

[6] "Pinging" is a fast, focused race walk in which plebes may not speak or interact with each other. It is the "moving version" of standing at attention.

ugliness I had never known. All traces of my makeup were gone with perspiration on the hot July day. My scalp burned, my stomach growled and the uniform was anything but flattering. For the girl who had spent her high school years reading fashion magazines, there was a solid, visceral misery about this whole situation. But something had already changed. Despite the way I looked and the discomfort I felt, I was already focused on surviving.

Now, as the noon hour approached, I faced the part of the day I dreaded most, the required "weigh in."

There were countless stations in the gym that day, just as there were outside on the Cadet Area. Medics stood on either side of me at the first stop, rolled my sleeves back and stuck several inoculation needles in my upper arms all at once in supreme efficiency.

I didn't flinch. I was too busy looking at the scale at the end of the gym.

Finished with the inoculations, I moved on to the next station.

A doctor checked my eyes.

Next station.

A dentist looked into my open mouth and lifted my tongue to peer underneath it.

Then, finally, the moment I had dreaded.

It was time to step on the scale.

My heart was pounding.

I stepped up to the scale in my sock feet behind two of my classmates. The fellow in front of me was enormous, a football player no doubt, with a body like a tank. He was soaked with sweat and, at a relatively early hour of the day, reeked of body odor. My instinct was to wrinkle my nose, but standing at the position of attention in front of the scale, I kept my face stoic. The scale nearly groaned as my classmate stepped onto the little square platform. Finally, he stepped off. I took my heart in my hands along with a deep breath and stepped forward.

I prayed to God that the morning's egg was light enough.

"What if I don't make it?" I thought.

My chest was tight. I could hardly breathe. My entire future loomed ahead of me.

I stepped up to the scale when ordered to do so and tried to feel thin.

The nurse slid the bar along the scale, made a note on the chart and then a check on the tag hanging from my shorts. I *had* to know the result. Stepping off the scale, I paused to look over the nurse's shoulder.

133 1/2 pounds.

I had made the weight requirement by a half pound.

I could have cried with relief.

"New cadets, eat up." said the firstie at the head of the table, "It's the last time you'll eat at 'fall out' for a long time."

Normally meals were continuing pressure for the New Cadets. We would learn to announce the foods at the table, memorize each upperclassman's beverage preference and who took what dessert so that we could carve the cakes and pies into the right number of perfectly matched pieces. We would also eat at the position of attention, back straight, one bite at a time with the fork placed on the plate at a 45 degree angle between bites. There would be no conversation between the New Cadets at the table save for what related to table duties.

For this meal, however, while we weren't allowed to speak to each other, we could eat freely and I nearly wiggled in my seat with anticipation. With the weigh-in successfully completed and the box checked, I looked longingly at the platter of ham as it was passed down the table. For weeks my diet had been comprised of raw vegetables and lean protein and I was starving.

When the platter arrived I made a fat sandwich, thick with ham and cheese and topped off with mayo. When the firstie at the head of the table looked away I took my first bite and reveled in the taste of the sandwich, nearly sighing with the satisfaction it brought.

"Sooooo good," I thought to myself with relief.

I had been so hungry.

We were sitting beneath the enormous mural depicting the history of warfare and I took a moment to examine its bright colors and shapes.

"Look ahead Cadet Bodeen," said the firstie, mispronouncing my name.

"Yes Sir," I responded.

At that moment I didn't care about his correction.

I was in love – in love with the fat ham sandwich on my plate and the wedge of chocolate brownie sitting next to it.

Many of the memories of R Day stayed with me for years. How could I ever forget standing in the locker room and the gym, taking off the hideous black shorts with the tags and donning for the first time the grey ME Trou,[7] the quintessential cadet uniform. I put my foot in each leg of the trousers and left my childhood behind.

As I changed, another female classmate was changing beside me and she took off her lovely pearl earrings, for new cadets were not allowed to wear jewelry of any kind.

"Hi, I know we haven't met," she said, "but I have to take off my earrings and I don't have anywhere to keep them. My parents gave them to me. Would you mind putting them in your bag?" she asked.

She took them off her ears and looked at them, obviously hating to part with them. I could see her predicament and agreed at once. The little pearl earrings were carefully placed in a small zipped pocket in my bag for safekeeping.

"I'll come find you and get them when things calm down," she said. They were beautiful real pearls and obviously had

---

[7] "Mock elastic trousers," lightweight warm weather grey uniform slacks.

sentimental value. I knew she would want them back and silently promised myself to keep them safe for her.

I never saw the girl again. In the insanity that is R Day, her face became a blur in a sea of faces that day and in the days that followed. Perhaps my face was a blur to her as well, for she never contacted me. For years I've kept the earrings, occasionally taking them out to look at them, wondering what happened to that young woman, where she is, what her life is like, if she ever graduated. With the earrings in the palm of my hand, R Day comes rushing back ... the tags hanging from my shorts, the din of the voices yelling across Central Area, the blur of 1400 stressed-out faces, all braving a system nearly two hundred years old.

Years later I had a conversation with someone who was not a grad but was fascinated by all that is West Point. He had read several of the books about past classes, attended West Point alumni group luncheons and so forth and considered himself something of an aficionado.

"I know what you went through," he said to me as we chatted.

We were in front of a coat check room at one such West Point function. The attendant handed me my coat and I put it on, feeling for my keys, shaking my head at the same time, feeling the kind of assurance that comes from knowing what someone else can't possibly grasp.

"I know what you went through," he continued, "and I really admire it."

"No ...." I replied, dismissing the compliment, "No you don't."

"No, really," he insisted, "I've done a lot of reading. I've talked to a *lot* of grads."

I shook my head.

"Let me tell ya," I said slowly, raising my gaze to his and meeting him eye to eye so that he could be sure of my intent, "The experience of being a cadet has an intensity about it that

I can't even begin to explain. Unless you have *been there, unless you have worn the M.E. trou, believe me,* you have no idea."

Without another word, I turned to go.

He didn't say anything after that. I think he knew better.

As the clock turned 1600 hours on the dot, the Hellcats,[8] looking as sharp as the cadets they played for, sounded the first drum. With the firsties in charge, my classmates and I stepped off in synchronous motion, through one of several sally ports[9] in Eisenhower Barracks, across the Apron and onto the Plain, marching to the music of the band. In just eight hours, the firsties had readied us for the first parade.

Pivot, step, pivot, step ...

Standing on the Plain in my new trousers and white shirt with the sweat running down my back, it was crystal clear that I was not in Kansas anymore. There was no nice straw man. No Toto. There was no love here, no nurturing or affection. No one here cared about Jenifer Beaudean's individuality or opinions or past accomplishments. They cared only about my towing the line and giving each and every task one hundred and ten percent. They cared about my becoming a soldier and eventually a leader of soldiers who would complete military missions as ordered while bringing my soldiers home in one piece.

In that moment however, standing on the grassy field in front of my parents and the rest of the American public, the fear and sweat and all that lay ahead faded away. Standing on the vast Plain among hundreds of my classmates, I felt only the wonder of being in this place. The voices yelling at my many blunders, the humiliating knee socks, even the weigh-in, all disappeared in this moment, beautiful and surreal. When it came time for the new cadets to take the oath, I held up my

---

[8] The Army band stationed at West Point plays for the Corps of Cadets during parades and events.

[9] A short tunnel leading from the cadet Areas to the Apron and onto the Plain.

right hand without hesitation and I felt the pride and enormity of joining this camaraderie, this legion of giants.

Our voices joined in unison pledging loyalty, service and honor. At that instant I felt the thrill of accomplishing the first few hours and I reveled in it. The sun beat down and the river of sweat made its way under my belt and beneath my trousers, but I ignored it and existed for the moment only *in* that moment and in the rhythm of the words as we all said them together. I hung onto it, knowing that in a second our hands would lower and the platoon would turn in step to the music and I would once again face this challenge that seemed overwhelming and strange. But at this instant, here and now, the moment and the accomplishment belonged to me. No one could take it away and I felt, despite my confusion and inadequacy, that I was in precisely the right place.

4

"Is that you New Cadet Beaudean?"

Cadet Percy's voice sang out down the hallway. He made a little song out of the end of my name, giving it three extra syllables. Barely across the threshold of my room, I pinged to the wall, turned on my right foot and looked far down the hall to see my nemesis sitting on a chair near the latrine, as if patiently waiting for me to appear. It was the third Sunday of Beast Barracks and our first free morning since R Day.

There was no choice but to acknowledge his presence.

"Yes Sir," I popped off with the obligatory reply to his greeting. I wished I could dart back into my room, but I had no alternative but to meet him head on.

"Did you square that corner? Get over here, Beaudean."

On his command, I raced down the hallway to where he was standing. Stopping in front of his chair, I performed a left face. I stood stalwartly at the position of attention, my back to the wall, my eyes straight ahead, wishing that the whole world would just go away. But Cadet Percy would not dissolve.

"Beaudean, every time I look at you, I wonder if you really should be here," he stated softly. "You want to go home, don't you Beaudean? You want to quit."

I looked at him, deep into his eyes.

Jackass.

"No Sir," I replied strongly.

Cadet Percy lived, ate and slept the Army, and he probably saw in me a new cadet who clearly didn't belong. Despite diligent effort on my part, my shoe shine was still substandard, my brass not up to par, and I suspect that he saw the low note of defiance in my eyes. As if this were not enough, despite the daily ordeal of meals under firstie scrutiny in the mess hall, I had already gained a few pounds since R Day.

I now weighed 138.

For a reasonably short woman, the five pounds already made a difference in my stature. For a firstie like Percy, a new cadet like me just didn't *look military*. He seemed set on making it his personal mission to make my life miserable. His room was only a few doors down the hall from mine and, like today, he often situated himself in the hallway on a chair with a tin of shoe polish, working on his already immaculate shoes, stopping new cadets whose duties forced them to brave the hallways.

Cadet Percy stood up and straightened his brass, which didn't need to be straightened.

"Do you see the funk in that belt buckle Beaudean?"

"Yes Sir," I replied sadly. How had I missed it? But alas, I had.

"Get out of here Beaudeaaaaan," he said, and waved me away, "and get back to your room and reshine your brass. It looks like crap."

I slammed through the door and my roommate looked up in surprise.

"I thought you were going to Chapel."

It was Sunday morning and new cadets who wished to do so were allowed to attend the Protestant service out to Trophy Point. Chapel was a safe haven. There would be no verbal corrections, no yelling on Trophy Point. It would be beautiful and serene and I would have five seconds of peace and quiet. In addition, it was rumored that there were cookies afterward and wasn't any situation made better with cookies? I knew that I needed to limit my food intake to control my weight, but the cookies sounded so good. I could practically taste the chocolate chips melting in my mouth.

Now, however, thanks to Cadet Percy, I had missed the formation.

"What the fuck is with that guy?" Jill asked after I relayed my encounter with Percy.

Jill was my roommate, my friend, my partner in crime, and helped me in more ways than I could count. Jill was the daughter of an Army colonel, had attended the USMA Prep School and was knowledgeable about all sorts of military tasks. We worked well together, weathering the storm, quizzing each other on our knowledge, sweeping the floor with the large square broom looking for "dust bunnies," making the beds together with their square corners and foldover exactly the width of a clipboard, cleaning the mirror with newspaper for a streakless shine and shining shoes until deep into the night with a towel stuffed under the crack below the door to hide the light from the upperclassmen patrolling the halls for violators of the lights-out policy.

With phone calls home still forbidden, she was my primary source of encouragement and there were many hours when I was grateful for her tutoring and quick wit.

"I think Percy's out to get me," I said sadly.

"Well fuck him," replied Jill with vehemence, "Come on, we'll put our gear together for tomorrow. Don't let him get to you," she said, seeing the wet in my eyes.

She grinned, "He's probably got a little pee pee."

I laughed so hard that my near tears of sadness turned to tears of mirth.

Hmmm, a little penis. Perhaps that was the problem with Percy.

I tucked that thought away for further consideration.

As it turned out, it was for the best that I didn't go to Chapel that morning because the tasks to get ready for Monday were endless. Jill and I worked all day shining our new boots and assembling our brand new BDUs,[10] then shining our shoes and brass for the haircut inspection in the morning. By the time the sun set behind the barracks, I realized that I had far

---

[10] "Battle Dress Uniform," or camouflage Army fatigues.

underestimated the time necessary to prepare for the next day. We had far to go before we would be ready.

As the clock rolled past "lights out" at 2330 hours, Jill and I toiled away, tucking the requisite towel under the crack in the door so that the firsties couldn't see the light on in our room. One of our squadmates had brought us both a few Fig Newtons from Chapel, and I chewed on my cookies, savoring the little fig seeds and the sweetness of them as Jill and I chatted over our chores.

Late into the night we worked, visited occasionally by members of our squad, all facing the same dilemma of too much to do in too little time. We all compared notes on the assembly of the rucksack and the LBE, or "load bearing equipment" that holds canteens and ammunition pouches. By the time the melancholy rendition of TAPS sounded across the barracks, I knew we were in for a long night. Jill and I looked at each other. We were sweaty and sticky on the sixth floor of a barracks without air conditioning. We were completely overwhelmed.

By one a.m. there was still no end in sight.

"The lacquer won't come off the corners of this brass,"[11] I lamented, looking down at the Academy crest, molded in brass and fitted for the front of our grey caps. I was completely mystified by how something that seemed so simple could be so stubborn.

"Y'know, I heard once that you can burn it off," mused Jill, more rhetorical than serious.

I didn't need another word of encouragement. By God, I was exhausted from the day and miserable. I needed a shower. I needed sleep. I needed to get the brass shipshape so as to avoid Cadet Percy's wrath. I was in no mood for an all-nighter and I had just about had enough of this no sleep bullshit. Without another word, I walked over to the floor where

---

[11] Hat brass was issued with a coating of lacquer covering it, which was rubbed off the brass to bring up the shine.

our gear was laid out and, taking the steel pot,[12] tore off the camouflage cover. Walking to the sink, I dumped the brass insignia into the basin that the helmet created, and poured in brass cleaner. Without another word, I looked at Jill with lifted eyebrows and a look that said, "Watch me now," and tossed a lit match it into the pot like a cavalier.

Within seconds, the flames were leaping up from the helmet cradled in the sink and Jill started to laugh.

"Holy shit Jenny," Jill choked.

"I'm starting an inferno," I replied, grinning "and you're laughing. Good thing you're not the fire safety officer."

I suddenly felt powerful.

Screw Percy, I'd burn the barracks down around him.

"I wish we had marshmallows," laughed Jill, watching the fire.

Sensing that we would soon need an extinguisher to put out the growing fire, I took a soaking wet towel and threw it into the steel pot, putting out the flames. Jill was now beside me and we peered together down into the helmet to see what had transpired. Sure enough, half of the lacquer had burned off. Elated, I needed no more encouragement. Suddenly the obstinate task seemed manageable.

"I swear to God, in thirty minutes I'm going to be in bed," I said to Jill.

Dumping a generous helping of the brass cleaner into the steel pot, I lit another match. The inferno ensued and we laughed uproariously as the flames did their work on the brass insignia. Clouds of smoke filled the room, but we were oblivious, so delighted were we by the prospect of the shortened task.

All was going according to plan, when suddenly, a fist sounded on the door.

BAM, BAM!

The sound of a firstie.

---

[12] Before Kevlar helmets, soldiers wore a steel helmet, or "steel pot,"on their heads when in the field.

"Quick, put it out," whispered Jill frantically.

I quickly threw the wet towel over the steel pot.

Instantly, we straightened up, assumed the position of attention and shouted in unison, "ENTER SIR!"

The door swung open and hit the doorstop with a loud thunk. The light from the hallway shone through the door, but the haze of smoke was so thick that it was hard to make out the figure of Cadet Percy standing in the doorway.

"What the HELL is going on in here?" Percy shouted, "Wait, no, don't answer!"

He tried not to cough from the smoke and fought back the instinct to wave his hand in front of his face. I could feel the corners of my mouth curling. Maybe he'd die of smoke inhalation. I could hardly stop the smile.

"Beaudean, you had better get that smirk off your face!" he commanded.

I worked hard at the corners of my mouth, willing them to droop, biting my tongue.

His voice took a sharper tone. "You two had better get in bed and I'd better not hear another noise from this fucking room, do you understand?"

Yes SIR!" we popped off together.

"GET in there!" his voice roared, and we leapt from where we were standing and in a single bound were under the covers. The door shut soundly behind him as he left, but we didn't dare leave our beds.

Jill snorted with laughter.

"Y'know, if we weren't in such deep shit, it would funny."

I laughed, "Yeah, well it's funny anyway." I drowned my giggles in the pillow.

"What are we going to do?" I asked my roommate wearily, looking at her through the smoky darkness. There were still tasks to be completed before morning.

Jill yawned, "Let's set the alarm for four o'clock."

"Right," I groaned, "Of course, why didn't I think of that? Four o'clock. Did I mention that I hate my life?"

I hated it ... but I was hooked.

5

"It's sadistic is what it is," I grumbled as I cleaned the soot off the sink and the mirror from the night's pyromania.

The Army is up and running by 5:20 in the morning. By seven a.m. the U.S. Army's soldiers have accomplished more than many human beings will accomplish all day.

This was hardly consolation as the alarm went off.

The firsties often played "wake up music." A speech given by General MacArthur in 1962 was one of the top picks. In the West Point world, MacArthur's words had become immortalized, a call to cadets and Army officers-to-be to become exceptional, honorable, duty-bound. The speech was beautiful, poignant and soul reaching. I loved its words, each one of them, along with the tempo of his voice, the call to duty. I loved it, but not at 0520. At this hour, I didn't give a crap who said what when. I wanted to go back to bed. I wanted caffeine. I wanted the hideous noise to stop.

We were due out at PT formation in minutes. As Jill and I reached the door to our room, we turned one at a time, dropping the upper edge of our shorts to give each other the legendary and ever impossible "dress off."

The dress off was a double fold achieved by pulling the excess material of the shirt at the sides, folding it back so that two nice, neat creases resulted where the back of the shirt tucked firmly into the shorts. To get a really good dress off required two people. One turned their back to the other and dropped the back of their shorts or trousers. Their classmate then pulled the sides of the shirt backward and held it in place while the first cadet pulled up their waistband, which then held the folds in place.

Theoretically.

The dress off was the bane of a new cadet's existence. Constantly scrutinized by the chain of command and never quite as perfect as that of an upperclassman, the dress off came undone with cheerful alacrity at every turn, folds unfolding, creases uncreasing, sending a new cadet hustling into the nearest classmate's room to have the dress off redone. The process was repeated ad nauseum throughout the day, the voice of a nameless firstie forever filling the hallway with this endless correction.

"Beaudean, you get in the nearest classmate's room and get a decent dress off!"

The result of the tightly folded shirt across the chests of the male cadets was a seamless, flawless look. Their pectorals stood out, accentuating the athletic perfection of these buff, fit tin soldiers. For the female cadets, the result was roughly the same, except that for a new cadet like me, a 36C breast size, the dress off made my chest look enormous. I was self conscious about my breasts anyway, feeling that they immediately made me look so entirely different than the rest of my squadmates, very voluptuous, very feminine, when really, at this point the goal was to go unnoticed and be "one of the guys." I despised the dress off.

These were the days I did not celebrate my place in the world as a woman, but instead, silently wished I were a man.

On this particular morning, Jill and I prepared to head out the door to P.T. formation, when the door burst open and out of nowhere appeared a frazzled, perspiring, stressed new cadet. We had never seen him before, but regardless of a lack of proper introductions, he put all formality aside, begging as if his life depended on it that Jill give him a proper dress off. Jill and I looked at each other in amazement.

Only here, in this place, could this whole scene unfold.

We could hear the first sergeant bellowing from the hallway.

"You'd better get back out here Davis. And that dress off had better be sharp."

Without a second glance, the unknown fellow turned around, placing his back to Jill, and dropped his shorts half-way down his butt, exposing a bit of the crack. Jill looked at me from behind our classmate and wrinkled her entire face. I marveled at how many different pairs of male underwear we had seen in the first few weeks of Beast Barracks, mostly ugly little white briefs. One had even been stained.

"Did you see those tighty whities?" I exclaimed to Jill in near disbelief, "I mean, for the love of God, would you not throw them OUT?!"

She nodded her assent with great vehemence and agreement. Really, men could be vile and disgusting creatures when you got right down to it.

Jill dutifully folded the back of the Gym-Alpha t-shirt of our harried classmate and with a *whoosh*, he was gone, only to be greeted by our company first sergeant, yelling his name in the hallway. We never saw him again. The entire transaction had transpired in moments with hardly a word exchanged between us. Anywhere else in the world this incident would be seen as utter nonsense or even sexual harassment. But at West Point, it was just part of the drill. In truth, we didn't need to know his name. We would have helped any one of our classmates who crashed through our door in desperation. They would do the same for us.

After all, as the saying went, *"Cooperate and graduate."*

I glanced sideways in the mirror as we sped with our squadmates out the door. I figured that it wasn't humanly possible for my chest to stick out any more. I inwardly groaned and hated my body. And the problem wasn't simply my ample breasts. My body was in agony. My chest and arms hurt, my legs ached, my feet were sore, my scalp was now peeling from the infamous home perm, my back and neck were broken out from sweating continuously. From various activities and athletics, my legs were nearly covered with quarter sized bruises. And I had gained seven pounds since R Day.

I was a complete mess and I felt like a fat, ugly little giraffe.

The irony about my burgeoning waistline was that for years new cadets had traditionally lost significant weight while at Beast Barracks. With the hazing that went on during meals, there was rarely time to eat, and with all of the physical exertion and fast metabolisms of fit men, loss of weight was expected. But the year that I entered the Academy, the fourth class system was enduring significant scrutiny and the firsties were under strict instruction to ensure that their new cadets maintained a healthy weight. In theory, this was a smart and humane idea. But for me, the 3500 calories per day designed for the male body and my own love of food made for a dangerous combination. No amount of athletics could compensate for the heavy meals we ate. And the seven pounds showed. There had been comments on my thick thighs and I knew that my weight gain had not gone unnoticed.

Out for a run one morning at PT, Percy had yelled at me from the back, "Beaudean, you can't possibly be gasping for air already. We've got three miles to go."

I knew that my curvier shape didn't help my athletic deficiency or the way that others perceived me. I had been the co-captain of the girls cross country team in high school, but now I was a small fish in a big pond and I could barely keep up. The seeds of self doubt began to take root. What began as a simple conversation with my well-meaning father, the words of a cross country coach, the voices of classmates and fashion magazines, began to grow into a self loathing that occupied my every day.

To be thin must be a great thing.

I began to believe that achieving the perfect body was worth any price.

141 pounds.

West Point is really a four year exercise in endurance. The prize does not go to the sprinters, but to those who can run the marathon, who can last through four exhausting years of military training, tough athletics and relentless academics. The summer at Beast Barracks did just what it was designed to do – it broke down the massive egos of a bunch of young overachievers and taught us what it means to follow. If we completed the summer and then plebe year, the system would begin to rebuild us, teaching us to lead with a sense of team, camaraderie and discipline. In every aspect of cadet life, the goal was to become a soldier first and then a leader of soldiers.

At West Point, military training is focused not only on building tactical competence, but also on learning strategic lessons from military leaders of the past that may help in future conflicts. Intramural sports, in which each cadet is required to participate, are designed to promote a fiercely competitive spirit useful on the battlefield. Academic rigors are intended to create soldier scholars. Classes steeped in quantitative learning will help them think critically and analytically.

Each new cadet who survived Beast Barracks and the four years that followed, would go on to an active duty commission in the US Army as a Second Lieutenant. Most would become, barely in their twenties, platoon leaders, responsible for the safety, training and welfare, of as many as 25 soldiers. The magnitude of the feat, to take a bunch of 18-year-olds and mold them into tactically proficient, fair and honorable leaders who could weather the pressure of combat, represented a significant task, but the West Point system of leadership development had been well honed over two centuries. The Academy consistently developed leaders of character, who would not only lead the Army, but the nation. What had started in 1802 as an institution to train engineers to build the new nation had developed into the most prestigious military academy in the world.

In the midst of this history and pride and dedication was me, perhaps in some ways the most unlikely cadet imaginable.

My family had no military history to speak of. My father's family had come from France in the 1860s and effectively avoided the American Civil War to establish their farms along the Mississippi River. Generations of Beaudeans had farmed there, but none had attended the Academy. My mother's family hailed from Ireland, Germany and Switzerland, and came to America after 1900. They settled almost entirely in New York City and had initiated an array of successful business ventures. But again, no military service. So unlike many of my classmates, I had no uncles who were West Point grads. My father was not a general. And, ironically, my mother was a pacifist.

But the odd fit between me and West Point didn't end with lack of family history in the Army. With the Academy's focus on engineering, again, I was an unusual fit. I was a bright student, but more a creative poet than an engineering genius. With the Academy's ever-present commitment to athletics, and particularly contact sports, I was a fish out of water. I had never played a contact sport in my life and was far from being a gifted athlete. Any athletic prowess I possessed was more the result of determination and guts than any real talent. I knew nothing really of what it meant to be an Army officer. I had never picked up a rifle. Finally, I fought an ongoing battle with my waistline, each day wishing I could eat every sweet morsel in sight while magically appearing in a body like the models in *Vogue* magazine -- lithe and thin.

So for me to become a cadet in a land filled with natural athletes, military sons and engineering marvels was really an odd idea. I could not have been more wrong for the part. But something about West Point had taken hold of me at an early age. I had seen this place from the distance of girlhood, holding my father's hand on a football Saturday. And even now, as I struggled to learn the basics, West Point worked its way into the fiber of my being.

In those first days, I reeled from many tough lessons in a harsh environment, but even with the voices yelling at me across the Area, inches from my face, commanding me, correcting me, and wearing me down, the mettle of my character rose in defiance and I swore that I would not give up. It never occurred to me during those first weeks to leave. Some of my classmates resigned, but I was determined to stay. If I were to leave, I would do it on my own terms, not as the result of Beast Barracks bullying. I determined to not let the system rule me. In the midst of what often seemed impossible, in the midst of a system that usurped individual will and identity, I determined not to lose myself. No matter what. And besides, with a helpful roommate to show me the way, perhaps I had a fighting chance at making myself a decent cadet.

Maybe I could be militarily proficient and respected.

Maybe I could develop into a fine athlete.

Maybe with work and practice I could become like my squad leader, fair and honorable, caring and competent.

And of course, most importantly, maybe I could be thin.

Years later, I was having lunch with a good friend at a little bistro in Paris.

"I would love to have a croissant today," she said to me with her rich French accent, "but I will have to eat light instead."

"It's a daily battle, isn't it?" I smiled in reply, "Not a day goes by that I don't think about what I weigh or what I'm eating. It's the never-ending and elusive quest of the western woman."

"It started for you in the military, no?" she asked.

I thought about it for a long minute.

"I'm not sure where it started," I mused, "But the one thing I'm sure of is that it's the same for every woman ... every woman I know thinks about her weight every day. I think that western women are surrounded by pressure to be thin, whether it's fashion magazines, or fitting into a certain size dress for a special occasion ... or just this continual need to be perfect."

"It is such a shame," my friend responded, "as there is so much good food to enjoy."

"True enough," I smiled in reply, picking at the lettuce in my salad.

Then a pause.

"We create our own hell," I said softly.

6

I looked down at my boots, properly laced, right lace over left, strides ahead of where they had been six weeks earlier. They were broken-in now, and comfortable. The repetition that makes up Army teaching had ingrained itself in the way my hands easily put the laces in their assigned spots, tying the ends and tucking them in the top of each boot. I had felt the change in myself over the six weeks. I now knew how to dress a wound, fire an M-16 and clean my M-14 parade rifle. I could configure my uniform properly and march in step. I was no longer the complete humiliation I had once been, but I would feel the effect of my slow start with my classmates for a long time to come.

Cadet Basic Training culminated with the new cadets sequestered at Lake Frederick, thirteen miles outside Washington Gate, for a week of training and frankly, a bit of fun. But the week was now finished and before nightfall we would face the full force of the Corps, all three thousand upper class cadets waiting to meet us back in garrison.

The next stage of New Cadet life was "Reorganization Week," or "Reorgy Week," the week prior to the academic year when the Corps mobilized for classes and living in garrison. Our morning thirteen mile roadmarch back to West Point proper would culminate with joining our academic year companies, each made up of roughly 160 cadets, with approximately forty in each class.

Now, with the Corps returning from summer training around the world, the fourth class would be outnumbered by the upper class cadets by a ratio of three to one. It would be a new world, with more than three times as many upperclassmen poised to correct our every move. The companies lived together, slept in the same barracks, trained together, played intramurals and drilled together. We would soon stress over learning nearly one hundred new names, each of their beverage preferences for meals, where their rooms were located and where they wanted their laundry placed. More importantly, we would learn who to avoid, who the biggest hazes were and how to navigate a system where the level of pressure went up several notches.

"The most important thing," my mother said, "is to find the bathroom."

The conversation occurred several years earlier. I was starting high school.

I looked up from where I was reading in some mild surprise.

"I know it sounds simple," she continued, looking down at the laundry she was folding, "but once you've found the bathroom, you're that much more familiar with the landscape. You now have one piece of critical information that you need. With this information, now you become more comfortable, because you're beginning to get your bearings. Each hour gets a bit easier, every day a little easier. Soon, it's a piece of cake."

You had to love the way my mother boiled it down to the basics.

Find the bathroom – or the latrine in this case, all amidst the yelling and corrections of one hundred upperclassmen in my new company area.

Could my mother's bathroom strategy be applied here? It seemed a stretch.

Before most eighteen year olds enjoying summer break had opened their eyes, the entire class of new cadets had torn down and packed up the camp, loaded their gear in their rucksacks and were now having breakfast to prepare for the thirteen mile march back.

I looked from my boots to the full tray of food that sat on my lap. An Army that lives on its feet must eat well to fuel itself, but I struggled with my love of food and just how many calories were truly necessary for the road march. My instinct and desire was to eat all of the eggs, the toast with its warm butter, the cereal and sausage -- to enjoy every mouthful. But surely this was more than enough calories for a young woman my size for an entire day. And even as I ate my meals, I felt self-conscious and watched, like I should not dare to eat. I don't know how much of it was imagined or how much real, but it further complicated my relationship with food.

I noticed my friend from another company eating only small bits of the breakfast. How would she have the energy for the miles ahead? More importantly, where did she find the willpower? I loved to eat, loved the smell and the process, the comfort of it. But with every bite I gained a little weight, a tiny part of a pound that began to add up. The exercise and exertion of the day hardly made up for the substantial calories provided by the Army, all geared for young men whose metabolisms were significantly faster than mine.

The coolness of the morning was a relief as I marched with my platoon through the woods. For several hours we walked, the morning warming around us. The companies filed through the woods along the golf course, a single file of nearly 1300 New Cadets, now close to Washington Gate. We entered West Point garrison and our cadre broke us out of our staggered line to form us into our platoons to march into post, past the cemetery, to the edge of the Plain, where we would finally pass the Superintendent's house.

The "Supe" was a three star general who lived in the most beautiful quarters on post, right beside the barracks. The brass played as we approached the Plain and we fell into step with the drum. The General stood on the perfectly kept, white porch of Quarters 100 and returned the salute of each company commander as we passed.

And then, without any further fanfare, the cadre marched us to our newly assigned company areas, where we would live for the next four years.

Or for however long I lasted.

For many, Reorgy Week would be worse than Beast itself. Academic studies had not begun and it was the worst scenario for a New Cadet – three thousand upperclassmen with time on their hands. They patrolled the hallways, chatting with each other, enjoying friendships built through months and years of living and training together. As they stood in the hallways, they examined the new cadets, stopping to correct an imperfect uniform or some other infraction. A New Cadet who left her room for a simple trip to the latrine might not make it back for hours.

"What's my name Beaudean?" asked an unfamiliar face with a strong voice. His brass was that of a yearling. He was clearly Italian or Greek in ethnicity, handsome in a roguish, rough kind of way -- and unbelievably short. At five feet four inches, I stood eye to eye with him. He looked at me with black eyes, waiting for a reply.

I had never seen his mug before and felt sure that if I had, I would remember. He had a mole above his right eye. It didn't really detract from his appearance, but despite the fact that I felt like an ugly duckling, I couldn't help thinking -- for God's sake, would you not have that thing removed?

All of this internal dialogue transpired in a millisecond as I trotted around my memory to see if I could dig up his name.

"I'm Cadet Denver, Boo-dean, and you'd better remember that name, do you understand?"

"Yes Sir," I popped off, not daring to correct his mutilation of my name.

"How do you pronounce your name?" he continued, as if reading my mind.

"Sir, Bo-dee-an," I sounded it out phonetically and putting the emphasis on the last syllable.

"Fine, Bo-dee-an," he sounded out, "Start The Days." He turned to go.

"Sir, the Days,"[13] I yelled, shaking the windows with my voice as I performed an about face and pinged along the side of the hall back to my room, "There are twenty and a butt days until Army beats the hell out of Holy Cross at Michie Stadium, there are ….."

Before I could get any further reciting the number of days to Christmas, 500th night and Graduation, Cadet Percy suddenly appeared at my side.

"Beaudean, are you still here?" he asked quietly as if he was pondering one of life's great mysteries.

I paused with my recitation and turned on my heel to stand at the position of attention in front of him. He was possessed, this man, I was sure of it.

"Yes Sir," I replied hesitantly, wondering where this conversation was going.

I sensed in him an apathy that was disturbing. My Beast squad leader had been tough on me and the rest of the squad, but she cared deeply about her troops, and I knew that for every ounce of effort I made, she noticed and encouraged me on to the next task. She wanted me to succeed. Cadet Percy, on the other hand, seemed to delight in failures, as if it fulfilled some unwritten prophecy of which only he was aware.

I later compared notes with Jill.

"You don't understand," I told my Beast roommate, "he's Satan incarnate."

"Listen, he can't be Satan," Jill replied, running a wad of newspaper across the mirror sprayed with window cleaner,

---

[13] New cadets are required to learn various pieces of information. Upperclassmen drill the new cadets on this "knowledge." Typical pieces of knowledge include descriptions of the branches of the Army, a thorough knowledge of the front page of the daily New York Times and the sports page, a series of daily counts called "The Days," and menus for meals. Some knowledge, once learned, does not change; other knowledge is revised daily.

"that would require some sort of devious thought and strategy. Some sort of brain. Percy is just an idiot."

"Yeah, okay," I replied sarcastically, "Idiot or not, he's got it in for me."

"Remember," said Jill, "little penis."

During those days I met with all sorts of trials. While delivering upperclass laundry, I inadvertently dropped Cadet Denver's dry cleaning three stories down the stairwell and was required to report to him several times over the course of two days as a result of the mishap. Each time there would be some new infringement. First my shoes were improperly shined. I could actually feel his breath in my ear while he discussed with me for fifteen minutes the importance of shined shoes and the proper discipline needed to maintain them. When I reported 45 minutes later with the same shoes, feverishly re-shined, Cadet Denver called in several of his classmates from the hallway to help him evaluate the improved spit shine. The upperclassmen circled me like wolves. The shoes were deemed "sad but acceptable for the moment," but by this time attention had switched to the shine on my brass belt buckle, which had a small bit of fingerprint on the upper edge.

"Beaudean, that's a fuckin' sorry mess on that belt buckle," said Denver.

"Yes Sir," I responded.

"I think we had better do a special tutorial on brass shining," Denver went on.

"Yes Sir," I replied miserably.

"How about 0520 hours tomorrow morning?" Denver asked.

"Yessir."

"Perfect," I thought as I performed an about face to leave his room, "I'll never sleep again."

In the midst of the stress of Reorgy Week, two events took center stage.

The first took place during lunch formation. I stood in my spot on the concrete, listening to the voices around me reciting their knowledge as the New Cadets stood in formation while the upperclassmen roamed around us.

"Did you see New Cadet Mayer?" one voice asked.

I didn't recognize who he was and it didn't matter.

"Yeah," another replied with a chuckle, "think her ME trou could be any tighter?"

Lisa Mayer was my classmate, a tall young woman with a fun personality, who, like me, had gained a few pounds during Beast. Her trousers were tight. So were mine. It occurred to me that similar things were likely being said about me. What had been intermittent disappointment with my body was evolving into a genuine loathing. To boot, I hated myself for my weak will. Why couldn't I just starve myself? I began to wish for the unthinkable. Could you make yourself anorexic? Was that an option?

Where did I sign up?

I tried to eat less at lunch.

The second event transpired the next morning. Cadet Denver opened the door in his ME trou, sock feet and his white undershirt.

"Good morning New Cadet Beaudean," he said.

He was calmer this morning, likely barely awake himself.

"Good morning Sir," I replied.

"Let's go out to the mirror," he said.

Each section of the barracks had a full length mirror right near the door to the outside, and we went and stood in front of it.

"May I touch you?" he asked.

There was no sexual innuendo here. This was the standard and respectful question asked before an upperclassman touched a plebe to fix a uniform infraction.

"Yes Sir," I replied.

He matter-of-factly moved my belt buckle a millimeter to the right.

"Attention to detail Beaudean, that's the key," he said.

He was actually trying to be helpful now.

"Any time you walk out to formation, you need to stop and look in the mirror and make sure that everything is in the right spot," he continued, "because then you can be sure that your uniform is immaculate before you go outside."

With a few more corrections, he dismissed me. The exchange had been relatively painless, but what Cadet Denver didn't know was that only part of my scrutiny was on my uniform. The rest was saved for my body. As he spoke I looked at myself in the mirror -- how my trousers sat on my hips, how there was a little pull of fabric here or a tiny bulge where I wished there wasn't. From that moment on, the mirror in the hallway became a part of my daily existence. Stopping in front of it several times per day, I would scrutinize my size and shape. Any focus on health was slowly and methodically replaced by near constant thought of my weight and wish to be thin.

Did the ME trou look a tiny bit looser today? Did my stomach feel any flatter?

Another seed planted.

Still 145 pounds.

7

Beaudean, how is the cow?" asked my squad leader.

"Sir, she walks, she talks, she's full of chalk ..." I recited.

I was standing in my spot, ten minutes prior to dinner formation as required. The evening was a bit chilly. It was nearly October. The Corps was steeped in academics. Life as a plebe was still intense and relentless, but there were small pleasures now – football Saturdays, Sundays with free time and phone privileges.

It was a beautiful evening and I had been given a few days of relative peace. There was a breeze across the Area as I stood in my spot with my classmates, waiting for the rest of the Corps to join us. I finished describing the cow's activities aloud and relished the few moments of calm while my squad leader chatted with a classmate. He had already forgotten about the cow and I was content to breathe the evening air and thank God for a few days without trauma. As I looked across the Area, I had to admit that West Point was downright surreal. The evening would have been notable for simply the beauty of the surroundings had it not been for one thing.

I would always remember that evening as the first time I saw Cadet Bailey.

Reorgy week and the weeks that followed had been so busy, frantic and stressful, that I hardly noticed the company first sergeant. I had heard about him, however. His legend preceded him. From a small town in Wisconsin, Cadet Bailey was among the oldest cadets in his class and it had apparently taken him several tries to gain admission to the Academy. He was not a particularly gifted student, but he was a warrior by nature, and West Point had been smart to accept him in the end. His meticulous focus came through in his military decorum, dedication to training, the way he handled himself and the relentlessness with which he pursued academics. Cadet Bailey applied himself with a vengeance and excelled at every turn, distinguishing himself as a cadet of high caliber and proving himself tactically proficient, militarily zealous, quiet, self-assured and inspiring. He was a born leader.

With many achievements to his credit, Cadet Bailey was assigned to the much-coveted company leadership position of first sergeant. He was responsible for the training of the company and for executing the direction of the cadet company commander. His uniform was flawless. His body was lean. He had just finished Army Airborne School with flying colors. He was completely squared away.

He also represented everything I was not.

That evening, like any other, the first sergeant strode out from the stoops to talk with one of his platoon sergeants, and I noticed him standing there, a quiet, stolid look about him. He was right in my line of sight, so I could observe him from the position of attention as I stood in my spot.

As he conversed, Bailey glanced up and saw me watching him but he simply went back to his conversation with his classmate with only a glance in my direction. He shifted his weight and I could see the outline of his legs. He was not particularly tall or handsome at first glance, but there was something about him that caught my attention and held it. I found my gaze glued to him, fascinated.

It wasn't long before I was in my own fantasy world where the cadet first sergeant was the hero and I was the damsel. I began to imagine that perhaps he noticed my stare and didn't mind it. Maybe he had seen my unattractive exterior and had sensed the deep and passionate woman within me. Maybe he was one of the few people in this environment who didn't hold looks as the primary measurement of personal value. Maybe he was secretly attracted to me from a distance. Maybe ....

As if hearing my thoughts, Cadet Bailey turned from where he was talking with the platoon sergeant and began an easy stride toward me. When we were shoulder to shoulder, he paused. I could feel him in my space, just inches away. From the corner of my eye, I could see his chest moving up and down in rhythm with his breathing.

"Cadet Beaudean," he said, pronouncing my name perfectly.

How did he know my name?

"Yes Sir," I replied a little breathlessly.

He looked at me, deep into my eyes, and our gaze held. I felt the hair on the back of my neck stand up.

"Why were you looking at me and not straight ahead?" he asked quietly.

I started to choke.

"No excuse Sir," I managed to articulate.

"That's right, no excuse."

He continued to look at me, and then, without missing a beat, said, "Beaudean, Start the Days."

"Yes Sir," I called, as he walked away, "Sir, the Days ..."

"LOUDER Beaudean!" called Bailey from the steps.

Later that week I spoke with my mother.

"I had cereal on my shirt yesterday morning. I have to report to my squad leader's room at 0520 hours tomorrow morning," I lamented on the phone.

I was at the pay phone in the sinks.[14] The air was thick with sweaty humidity as fourth squad, second platoon worked with weights and did countless pushups. Through the glass of the phone booth I could see their heads bobbing up and down as they pounded out the repetitions.

"Oh honey, you can master this West Point thing," my mother replied without missing a beat. I could tell by the lilt

---

[14] Basement area of the barracks containing gym lockers, weights for weight lifting, the Day Room (forbidden to plebes) containing the only company TV, and pay phones.

in her voice that she had the phone stuck between her shoulder and her chin, probably stirring homemade spaghetti sauce.

I could see it. Smell it.

"Besides," she continued, "you need your sleep. You just tell your squad leader that you can't stop by."

She expressed this thought as if I was declining a request to bake cookies for a church function. I imagined what the statement would sound like coming out of my mouth.

"Sir, I'd love to stop by tomorrow morning at 0520 hours, but my mother says I need more sleep, so I can't make it."

Good God. Can you imagine?

I'd be hanging from the clock tower by my feet.

Despite my mother's rather naïve view of life as a cadet, my parents were a tremendous support. My father was ever the encouraging voice, and I sped to the mailroom on many a day to look in my mailbox and smile with delight at the arrival of a note from my father. My mother, pacifist though she was, did her best to be enthusiastic about my military training and development. They visited whenever possible. Already, we had shared a picnic or two on Trophy Point with several of my classmates invited to share sandwiches and cake.

It was Wednesday and the week was nearly finished. I looked forward with great anticipation to the coming weekend when my parents were planning a visit. Face-to-face visits trumped phone calls and letters by a long shot. With the eager banter of my parents, the clever silliness of my sister, a visit was salve to my fourth class wounds. It took me away from cadet life, even if only for a few minutes. I missed the backyard wiffleball games with my father and the long philosophical discussions with my mother. I missed the affection and difficulty and all of the idiosyncrasies that made the good and bad of life with my family a familiar pain.

Until the weekend, I faced each day with trepidation. I desperately wanted to see my family. Bottom line – I needed to lay low and fly below the radar for the next couple of days.

I left my room that morning, committing myself to staying out of trouble in order to protect my weekend free time. I promised myself a perfect day.

But the day had other plans.

According to plan, the first hour of the morning went without a hitch. I had memorized the sports section and even surprised my squad leader with my command of the baseball scores as the American League headed toward the playoffs. Breakfast was uneventful. There was a huge test in Electrical Engineering later that morning for the second class and the cows were consumed with quizzing each other in preparation.

Occupied cows meant happier plebes.

The table duties were carried off in perfect harmony. The upperclassmen had nothing to legitimately correct and left us alone. But what I didn't know was that there was a storm brewing ahead ... and its name was Percy.

At 0720 hours, the day began to unravel.

I had always been relatively lucky when it came to academics. I was a "quick study," and even with advanced classes in high school, I succeeded with relative ease.

This, however, was a different world -- all bets were off.

West Point's academic program was designed to be tough for every cadet, regardless of ability level. Calculus, of which three semesters were required, was organized by aptitude and cadets were grouped into sections of roughly twenty classmates with similar test scores. Once the first major test of the semester was graded, the cadets were shuffled based on their average in the class, so that cadets were continually taught and tested at their own performance level. For those who scored high and were in the overachieving section one, the professor tailored the class to challenge them. For those struggling in the lower sections, again, the class was designed to push their ability level.

Either way, you were screwed.

I began the semester in Calculus Section One. How this happened, I could not imagine. Even as a bright student, mathematics had never been my strong suit. My days as a straight A student were long gone now and I struggled to keep up with the pace of the high achieving class. After the first WPR,[15] the sections were shuffled and I went very quickly from the overachieving section one to the much less impressive section twelve. Jill struggled endlessly with her studies and, as we reshuffled after the first exam and found our new classroom, we looked at each other across the room and simultaneously rolled our eyes.

Ahhhh, the suffering.

As if the class itself were not difficult enough, math class was its own form of haze. When the "P"[16] gave the command "Take Boards," we rose and took our places at the blackboard behind their chair. We measured off our workspace using a long straight edge and piece of chalk. When finished, the board boasted two boxes in the upper left hand corner, neatly measured and outlined in white, filled in with our name and section or problem number. There was also now a vertical line running down the exact middle of the board, so that there were two writing areas, left and right. The professor then gave each of us a calculus problem to solve, which we began to work through on our board. Eyes were not to drift. Cadets were expected to focus on only their own board and not their neighbor's.

Generally the exercise was timed. Answers were double underlined in red chalk. At the close of the exercise, a selected cadet would present their results to the group with a long pointer, standing to the side of the board so as to create a professional presentation.

Painful at 0720 hours.

---

[15] "Written partial review," major exam.
[16] Cadet lingo for "Professor."

As I willed my Wednesday to continue its flawless beginning, the instructor called on me.

"Cadet Beaudean," said the P, as I stood in front of my board space, which was neatly written and, I was convinced, completely wrong.

"Yes Sir."

"Would you please present to the class your answer to the second problem?"

"Yes Sir," I responded, and picked up the pointer.

I dutifully stood to the right of my board, and using the pointer, went over the steps of the problem. I finished and waited for the P to correct my logic, or lack thereof.

"Cadet Beaudean, you lost your way on step three and perhaps this is a good time to revisit that step with the group, so let's take seats and make sure we're understanding how to properly solve this type of problem. Cadet Beaudean, good job on your presentation, despite the fact that your answer was incorrect. I do want to remind you however that a proper and serviceable uniform is required in this class."

I looked down at where he was staring at the big blob of oatmeal on my tie.

I blushed and took out my handkerchief to dab at the cereal.

Cereal again! Damnit! It was always something.

I received a grade of D for the day.

Super.

"Focus Jen, it's not the end of the world," I consoled myself as I sped from Thayer Hall to the gym for the legendary Phys Ed class, Gymnastics, "Positive thinking is the key to success."

I changed into my gym alpha uniform with the rest of my classmates and looked in awe at the instructor demonstrating the latest skill.

Hell had a new name – "Spaztics."

Cartwheels and handstands had once been child's play in the front yard on a summer day, but now these playground skills were a highly practiced and precisely graded nightmare. Buff and perfectly built Army instructors, immaculately dressed in tailored athletic shorts and t-shirts, demonstrated a tumbling skill. The demonstration included the techniques and characteristics of a perfect stunt, like a handstand, a cartwheel, or climbing a rope twenty feet up. The instructor then demonstrated the undesirable, the inept, the grossly inadequate characteristics that a would-be gymnast might demonstrate instead, earning the cadet a much lower grade. A score of five for a skill meant mastery of the task. To receive a five was ridiculously rare. A score of a three was passing, and an instructor could even grant a "high three" or "low three" to further emphasize the nuance to which the plebe had mastered, or not mastered, the task.

The day's task was the headstand and I looked on with a combination of amazement and dread as the instructor demonstrated the skill, wondering if it was even possible for me to pull off such a move. It was at times like this that I felt acutely self-conscious about my weight. If only I were thinner, maybe all things would be possible.

If only I were skinny …

145 pounds.

My classmates and I now broke into teams to practice the skill for 10-15 minutes, and then came together for the grading session. When it came my turn, the instructor stood in front of me with a clipboard.

"Alright Miss Boo-deen," she mispronounced, "Please execute your headstand."

I tried to be optimistic as I looked at the instructor in front of me.

Her arms were ripped, her legs sculpted, and her body reflected athletic prowess. She was a superhuman Amazon from the netherworld. Me? I was in my gym alpha uniform, with a proper dress off, breasts sticking out, thighs a bit on the heavy side, and really, truth told, nothing sculpted anywhere. I thought of my bigger-than-I-liked ass in the air and wanted to cringe.

"Now this is where positive thinking is key. It's not about looks," I told myself with energy. I reached into my soul for a dose of determination and stood on the mat in my clunky, white "stars & bars" sneakers. The instructor gave me two practice tries, which didn't go too badly.

"Miss Boo-deen, you need to hold the position," the instructor suggested, stating the obvious as I flopped over unceremoniously.

I listened attentively to her suggestions, silently willing my enthusiasm to translate into an actual headstand. As the instructor held the sharp little pencil over the clipboard, I took a deep breath. Bending my knees, I put my hands flat on the mat as instructed, elbows on the insides of my thighs. Reaching down slowly, I put my forehead on the mat, and began to lift my butt up over the tripod that my head and hands created.

For exactly one second I was vertical, and then with a thunderous FLOP, I landed flat on my back, now gazing up at the ceiling. The instructor leaned over me, looking into my face.

"Miss Boo-deen – that's a high Zero."

"She gave me a high *zero*," I told Jill ruefully as we shined our belt buckles for lunch formation. I had been assigned a new roommate for the semester but I made it a practice to stop by Jill's room whenever possible. It was either that or deal with my over-zealous roommate's relentless and loud recitation of daily knowledge while I yearned for peace, quiet and privacy.

"Now I have to go for Additional Instruction in *Gymnastics* for God's sake," I continued.

Jill nodded her head in empathy.

"God, I hate that fucking class," she said, shaking her head. She was moving the t-shirt over the brass in little circles. "Hey, I can't get this mark off," Jill said, musing over the buckle, "Would you mind taking that bundle of laundry to Percy? He'll kick my ass if he doesn't have it by lunch."

I looked at the clock. My uniform was ready, the oatmeal gone from my tie, and upon review in the mirror I actually thought I looked pretty good. If I hurried, I could make it into Percy's room and back before he came back from class.

"Sure," I said, and placing my hat on my head and the bundle under my arm, headed for the door.

Jill, meanwhile, was still scowling over the buckle, and didn't look up, for if she had, she would have seen the back of my trousers.

8

Blissfully unaware of the trouser situation, I pinged down the hall to Cadet Percy's room, determined to dump his laundry and make for greener pastures before he returned. What I had not counted on was that Cadet Percy's Juice[17] class had ended early. Stopping at his doorway, I performed a left face, and looking at the door, knocked several times. Whether Cadet Percy didn't hear me or whether I didn't knock loud enough we'll never know. Assuming the room was empty, I opened the door with a *whoosh* and made a bee-line for Percy's foot locker to drop off the bundle.

There he was, standing in front of his wardrobe in his underwear. Stunned, I instantly dropped the laundry, gasped and blushed crimson to the roots of my hair.

"Holy shit Beaudean," yelled Cadet Percy, grabbing his trousers, "get outta here!!"

I raced to the door and jerked it open so hard that it bounced against the doorstop. I rushed through the doorway without even a glance to what was ahead and plowed headlong into Cadet Bailey. My impact with the first sergeant was so substantial that it nearly knocked me off my feet. Pandemonium ensued. Cadet Bailey felt the impact of my momentum against his chest and dropped his hat, falling back a step while I slammed against the wall. As I tried to right myself I reached for his hand for balance before I realized with horror what I was doing and yanked my hand back.

Bailey gave me a dark look and reached down to recover his hat.

---

[17] Electrical Engineering.

As he leaned over and I straightened myself the hilarity of the scene hit me -- Cadet Percy, my nemesis, in his underwear, my speedy departure, my collision course with my romantic interest in the hallway. I was horrified, and yet, how could this not be funny?

I couldn't help it. I started to laugh.

Cadet Bailey, however, was not amused. Within a second he straightened and composed himself and stepped forward, about to rip me a new one in no uncertain terms. I choked as my laugh morphed instantly to fear. I came to the position of attention in an instant and looked at him, chiding myself silently for my lack of military bearing. I sucked my breath in and held it for what I knew was coming.

"Plebe year is kind of a game."

I was visiting West Point as a high school student, spending the day shadowing a yearling. I was already in love with the idea of being a cadet. It looked so extraordinary and amazing from the distance of teenage civilian life.

"What do you mean a *game*?" I asked my escort.

"Well, as long as you play the game ... learn your knowledge, execute the military training, do your duties, then it's almost kind of fun, and there are a lot of moments of humor, even with the upperclassmen."

"Hmmm," I thought, tucking that away for future reference.

"One thing though," he continued, and gave me a long look, "If you act like it's a game, and they see it ... then it's not a game anymore."

Standing in front of Cadet Bailey, there was no game.

"What do you think you're doing Beaudean?!" he asked, in the same tone and volume he used to call the company to attention. My ears flamed red.

"Sir," I stammered, "No excuse Sir."

Because my back was not quite against the wall, Bailey could see the back of my uniform and he started to wag his head. His look changed and he actually looked like he felt sorry for me.

It occurred to me at that moment that something was wrong, even more wrong than my momentary breach of protocol.

"Beaudean," he said quietly, "you need to go back to your room, pull yourself together and clean off the back of your ME trou, okay? Before formation!"

And without another word, he turned on his heel and walked away.

As if a horse breaking from the starting gate, I bolted madly back to Jill's room. Charging through the door I called desperately to my friend, "What the hell is on my pants?!?!"

"Oh Christ Sweetie, do you have your period?"

My face fell with utter mortification.

How was it possible that I had walked around for God knows how long that morning with my period bleeding through my trousers?! If only someone had said something. Surely someone had seen it.

How could they not say something?

What a nightmare! On top of the humiliation connected to the incident itself, it *had* to be Cadet Bailey who saw me. As if my embarrassment were not enough to bear, it was laundry day and we had just sent our other lightweight trousers out to be cleaned. I had to wear the stained trousers or go naked. To top it all off, lunch formation with haircut and uniform inspection was just twenty minutes away. Could the scenario get any worse? I wanted to throw up.

Jill, thankfully, was not to be defeated, and good and faithful friend that she was, she ran a sink full of cold water while I took off the trousers and went to town with her spot remover. Standing there, we alternately held the hair dryer on the spot, while I described in great detail Cadet Percy's pose in his underwear.

"Oh my God, I'm going to wet my pants," howled Jill as she laughed uproariously.

Her laugher was contagious and I joined my friend in hysterics, tears running down our cheeks, me in my underwear, holding the hair dryer on the wet spot while Jill held the trousers.

"So no view of his pee pee?" she asked with a laugh.

"No, but there he was, looking like a Greek statue," I continued, giggling through the tears running down my cheeks.

"Oh my God, oh my God," howled Jill, "Oh, stop, stop, my stomach hurts."

It felt wonderful to laugh. A release.

We finally quieted as it came time for me to go out and take my place as Minute Caller. I took a long look at my friend.

"Thanks for being there," I said quietly.

"You betcha, wouldn't miss it," my friend replied.

I pinged out to my spot in the hallway on the second floor and, standing at the position of attention, called the minutes ticking down to formation. At the last call, I turned and raced down the stairs, out the front door and down to formation.

At the command to expand the ranks for haircut inspection, the squads stepped apart. As luck would have it, to add to my "perfect" day, the commander, Cadet Vastner, well known for his toolish ways, and my new friend Cadet Bailey, had chosen my platoon to inspect.

I could see Cadet Vastner out of the corner of my eye. He was tall, had a massive chest, and was very blond and Arian looking. Rumor had it that he was head over heels for the captain of the women's tennis team. This had been big news when the rumor came to light, because apparently, for the first three years of cadet life, Vastner swore never to date a female cadet. Cadet Bailey, shorter and less visible, stood beside him and made notes of the commander's corrections as the two looked over the platoon's haircuts and uniforms. Nothing was to be out of place and no one was above the inspection scrutiny, regardless of rank. Cadets Vastner and

Bailey, with their combined and relentless attention to detail, would make sure of it.

Cadet by cadet, they made their way through the platoon.

"Ready, Step," said Cadet Vastner quietly, and he and the first sergeant turned a right step in harmony and a left face to stand in front of me.

By the grace of God, Cadet Vastner seemed to be in a good mood. He looked over my shoes and uniform while my eyes stared straight ahead, resting on the middle of his ridiculously large chest.

That day I weighed 146 pounds. I wondered if he thought I was fat.

Cadet Vastner said to me in the voice of someone who doesn't really care but feels compelled to ask, "Beaudean, how are things going?"

Today of all days, to ask this question, seemed ironic.

I looked him in the eye, as I answered the requisite, "Fine, Sir."

"Academics okay?"

"Yes Sir," I answered.

"Good, keep up the good work," said Vastner, concluding with his standard line of encouragement for the fourth class.

"A politician in the making," I thought.

"Ready, step," he commanded.

Cadet Vastner stepped ahead to the next cadet to my left, leaving in front of me, eye to eye, Cadet Bailey.

I looked into the first sergeant's eyes and was immediately lost in the events of the morning. Standing there, I felt all of my inadequacy and embarrassment whirling around me. The first sergeant was so perfect, his uniform and his body so made for the part. Whereas I was the kind of cadet who goes to Calculus class with oatmeal on her tie, who flops like a large fish during spaztics class, who runs around with her monthly cycle emblazoned on the back of her trousers, losing her military bearing at the first obstacle. To top it all off, I sensed that my weight was always at the center of my inadequacy. In a society that praises the perfect female form, whatever that means, the standards of thinness were even more harsh at West Point. In a place where one could never be strong enough, fit enough, or thin enough, I stuck out with all of my gross inadequacies and I knew it. I figured Cadet Bailey probably marveled that I had lasted this long.

As he stood in front of me, Cadet Bailey looked at me with a long stare. Our eyes were locked and it felt different than simply the first sergeant looking over one of the company plebes. There was a connection of some sort and I stood there in confusion, wondering what was crossing his mind. Did he see that I really wanted to succeed? Or was he like the others, who could not see past my faults. Cadet Bailey said nothing. I moved my eyes and focused on the rank insignia on the collar of his shirt, trying to control my breathing. At the last moment, I looked up. The first sergeant was looking at me. Our eyes met again.

There it was. Something.

My pulse pounded in my neck, and then the moment passed as the two leaders moved on to the next squad.

The hour after lunch was free of class or other obligation. I decided the events of the morning warranted a break, so I sat in the quiet of my room with my feet propped up on my bed, lost in *Vogue*. Outside my window I could hear the voices of the upperclass cadets walking across the Area and my mind wandered to those who had gone ahead of us -- the greats -- Lee, Grant, Eisenhower. I looked at the fall fashion issue and thought about how different the world was now and how different West Point was with me in it.

I eyed the Snickers bar sitting in my desk drawer. I hid my boodle[18] now, assuming that any cadet who saw my snacks, whether classmate or upperclassmen, would see me as the fat girl snacking when she should be working out. Hiding the food and its extra calories somehow negated that it existed.

---

[18] Cadet slang for treats and snacks — cookies, candy, etc.

Maybe if I hid the candy bar and hid my eating it, it would stay away from my already round posterior.

The snickers peeked out at me from under a notebook on military tactics. I couldn't resist and tore it open. It was only 250 calories. It was quiet in my room and I had privacy to munch away, savoring the chocolate. No one saw it, so it didn't count.

I weighed 147 pounds.

Military and professional development classes were held in the top of Washington Hall. The lower section of Washington Hall held the six wings of the mess hall, complete with an enormous mural that depicted the history of warfare, and stained glass windows. The tower that rose from the center was filled with classrooms. My afternoon class was on the sixth floor, so I reluctantly finished the chocolate, concealing the wrapper in a tissue so that no one would notice it in the trash can. Placing the magazine in my desk drawer, I placed my grey cap on my head and left the solace of my room.

Today's lecture in Military Tactics class was on creating a final protective fire for a platoon perimeter using an M60 machine gun. The gist was that if your perimeter was being overrun, the machine gun fire was aimed across the front of the perimeter to protect the troops as the platoon pulled back. I found the class moderately interesting, but also figured that if you ever had to use this tactic, it meant that your position was being overrun by the enemy and you were basically fucked. With this analysis, my mind wandered back to Cadet Bailey, lost in daydreams, and my eyes grew heavy.

"Cadet Beaudean, would you please stand up?" the professor asked sternly.

Cadets traditionally stood behind their chair if they felt themselves getting sleepy during class. As the lecture ended, the P lectured me sternly on the essential nature of military tactics class and also the self discipline that helps a cadet know when they need to stand up so that they can stay awake and absorb the essential information. The P droned on and the minutes ticked away. I fought off the instinct to fidget and waited patiently with an occasional "Yes Sir" until he was finished.

This day really was not turning out as I had planned.

The days were already getting shorter on the Hudson and the evenings were cool.

"TAKE SEATS!" came the command from the Poop Deck and we all sat down to dinner.

Four thousand chairs scraped in unison and we all sat down. My classmates and I busied ourselves filling each upperclassman's glass with their preferred amount of ice and drink, and cutting the dessert into perfectly neat wedges. One responsibility of the fourth class was to announce how many servings of each dish remained on the table, and as the fish were not a very well liked entrée, there were at least five left over. Hoisting the tray up over my left shoulder as the duty required, I began the recitation.

"Sir, there are five and a butt[19] servings of baked cod remaining on the ..."

Cadet Percy was eyeing me from the other end of the table, obviously remembering the day's x-rated incident. As the words came out of my mouth, my lips began to crack just the smallest hint of a smile.

"BEAUDEAN, are you smiling again?" one of the cows yelled down the table. He was pissed.

The gig was up and I instantly set the large tray of fish on the water pitcher, which was positioned to my left, on the corner of the long table. It was a precarious setup and looked suspiciously like the leaning tower of Pisa with a flying saucer on top.

"YES SIR," I called in response to the upperclassmen.

---

[19] The rule is that there are never exactly five servings, so a plebe announces the dish as "five and a butt" remaining, meaning "five and a little."

As I turned to address him, the edge of my shoulder caught the tray and a cascade ensued. Over the platter went, and with it the pitcher of water, and as if perfectly coordinated, the five remaining codfish slid off the tray wholly and neatly into a large pitcher of lemonade, which my fellow plebes had placed on the floor.

The blood drained from my face as pandemonium ensued.

The pitcher of water had just missed my classmate and now covered the floor while the pitcher clanged against the slate. Upperclassmen from surrounding tables had risen to survey the damage and clap. The five pieces of fish were now bobbing gracefully in the big pitcher of lemonade, the platter and the sauce were on the floor, and all hell was breaking loose. The two yearlings at my table were in hysterics. The two plebes with whom I shared table duties were torn between keeping a straight face and being obviously horrified. The cows went ballistic and I knew that death by hazing was upon me.

Cadet Percy, meanwhile, had obviously had quite enough of young Cadet Beaudean for one day

"BEAUDEAN," he barked, "Report to my room after dinner!"

"Yes Sir," I cried, my horror and dismay mixed with a desire to laugh at the scene around me. I looked down at the fish now floating in the pitcher of lemonade and fought to keep my composure.

It was the stuff that *I Love Lucy* was made of. I knew that if I didn't keep it together I would pay heartily.

"Beaudean, I have to say ..." began the yearling seated next to me.

"Yes Sir?" I asked.

"Well Beaudean, at least you returned those fish to their natural habitat."

That was all it took. I lost it.

"It's not even that you dropped the fish, which is unbelievable really if you think about it. I mean, really Beaudean, what were you thinking? You had some fucking engineering marvel built on the end of that table!" yelled Cadet Percy.

We were in his room and the concrete walls were nearly shaking with his anger.

If I had been a cartoon, his volume would have blown my hair back. I had never seen him so angry. His lips were red for God's sake and I wondered if he was entirely well.

"On top of it, as if the water, the fish, the lemonade, and nearly drenching your classmate weren't enough, you then proceed to laugh out loud ... not even stifling it, but *out loud* for fuck's sake. Where is your military bearing?"

"Yes Sir, No Sir," I replied, confused about which accusation to address first.

There was a pause and I felt the weight of it, hanging in the room. I could see the process in his face as he decided what measures to take.

"Do you have plans for the weekend?" asked Cadet Percy. There was an evil glint in his eye and my heart began to sink.

"Yes Sir," I replied slowly.

"Well, you don't anymore," he said.

I felt the world spin around me and my sharp intake of breath must have alerted Percy that he had driven the knife home.

"Beaudean, you're dismissed, and if you're smart, you'll stay clear of me for a while," finished the firstie.

"Yes Sir," I replied, and executing an about face, made for the door.

There would be no visit with the family that weekend.

I went to bed that night immediately, blowing off my studies and wanting only to feel the safety and solace of being under the covers.

Jill appeared in the doorway with a mysterious package tucked under her arm.

"C'mon, let's drown our sorrow," she said and took out a plastic cup.

Definitely not a game.

9

I looked at the calendar on my desk and it read December 11th. I stood with cookie in hand, munching away while I marveled at the miracle that was my first completed semester at West Point. I had survived Beast Barracks, Reorgy Week, plebe "spaztics" class, Cadet Percy's malevolence and differential equations calculus. It was a damned miracle. The real world seemed distant, far away. I wondered if I would even recognize normalcy, or a day without the hazards of plebe life.

Exam week passed, but the toll it took was heavy. West Point academics are notoriously tough. Each semester there are those who will not return thanks to exam week. When I was a cadet, very few overachievers scored straight A's. Even now, people mention to me that they had a 3.8 GPA in college. At West Point, I didn't even *know* anyone who had a 3.8. Every assignment, every class was graded on a bell curve, with the bulk of the class achieving a C. And every semester, the Academy's relentless academics took its toll and some failed out. Thankfully, I wasn't one of them, at least that semester.

The day of departure dawned and I looked around the room. The beds were stripped of linens, their striped ticking running parallel to the walls. Empty and quiet, the room reflected how I felt ... enormously relieved that I had survived to this point, but so unsure of myself, so full of angst and empty with exhaustion.

I listened to the hum of the Corps around me, the sound of upperclass cadets talking in the Area, trashcans being put in doorways so that a female cadet could be in a room with a

71

male, brooms full of dust bunnies being cleaned out in the hallway upstairs. I was a part of the hum now -- part of the hum, but desperate to go home.

The chain of command was undoubtedly planning for the next semester and the oh-so-toolish company commander, Cadet Vastner, and his first sergeant, my admire-from-afar love interest, Cadet Bailey, must have met like every other commander and first sergeant before them. Maybe Vastner was thinking more about his romance with the captain of the tennis team than he was assignments. Maybe nobody cared where I landed. I have a suspicion, however, that I was the "troublesome plebe" or perhaps even the "fucking pain in the ass plebe" who needed a great deal of work. My guess is that the chain of command wagged their heads as they thought of me and tried to determine what strong cadre to assign me to and where to put me so I might actually get some military decorum through my thick head.

As I put the last touches on my room and grabbed my bag to head out the door, my new assignment for the next term was far away and distant. All I could see ahead was two weeks of waking up without stress, with no newspapers to deliver, no Calculus class at 0710 and no knowledge to recite. If I had known what the next term would bring, perhaps I wouldn't have been quite so happy, but I was innocently oblivious and there was little that could put a pall on fourteen well-earned days of leave.

The door to the stoops opened and then crashed closed as I pinged onto the little stone porch, down the steps, past the clock tower. There was a light snow on the ground and patches of the Area peeked through, the little marks fading where the squads had stood during the last formation of the term.

I rounded the corner of Grant Hall and cadet life was suddenly at my back. I could see my father standing in the distance. The car was pulled up as far as it could go and it was still running as he stood waiting for me.

I can still see him there now.

His hands are in his pockets, a cheerful anticipation about him as he looks for me. His eyeglass frames are too large for his face, outdated. With his puffy blue coat, ten years old, and his worn loafers, he is clearly a man focused on something other than appearances. He is neat and put together, as always, but the clothes show significant wear. He is a little geeky, but it is endearing. I know him to be a tremendous human being, extraordinarily respected in the community and among his fellow scholars, and unaware of what it means to have an enemy. He stands there even now in my memory, holding in his heart not only his anticipation of my time at home, but all the fine hopes that a devoted parent harbors for the child they love.

Plebes stopped pinging once they hit the edge of the cadet area and I slowed my pace. When I first spied him, he was looking at the height of Mahan Hall and at the windows of Grant Hall. My father was a man fascinated by every aspect of life. I sensed that he had missed me while I was away, but I also knew that he shared my every victory, however small, and felt the pain of my every heartbreak. I think he lived vicariously through me during my days as a cadet. If he had the chance to live a second set of choices, he might have applied to West Point himself.

He turned his head and saw me coming toward him and his face lit up in a wide grin. He clasped me tightly and said something like, "Hey kidnick," one of his many nicknames for me, along with "goober peas," which, by the way, refers to peanuts. Taking my bag, he opened the trunk and set it inside, and we got in the car. The profound relief I felt leaving Post, driving out through Thayer Gate, was palpable. Just the thought of waking at my leisure in the morning -- nowhere to go, nowhere to be, no uniform to don, no upperclassman to report to -- was better for the soul than chocolate. The miles rolled away and my father queried me about the latest comings and goings. He knew the names of some of the upperclass cadets and some of my classmates. I marveled at how he kept up with it all. For over six months, he faithfully kept abreast of all the drama associated with my life as a plebe. Chatting happily, we shared the elation of six months finished.

"Really, getting this far is an accomplishment," he said, nodding as he said it, watching the road.

"You have no idea," I thought.

Without another word I fell asleep against the car window.

Christmas leave lasted two weeks and the days swept by like a landslide. Little had changed. I stood in the kitchen in my slippers, stealing a cookie here and there, the war continuing between my wish for a magic road to thinness and my yearning for Christmas sweets.

The real world felt familiar but strange. Even as the family prepared for Christmas, I felt a part of it, but oddly separated, as if I knew things that the rest of the world did not. For the moment, however, I was swept up in the cozy house and all of its holiday preparation.

The rock solid tradition of the Army had nothing on the Beaudean household. My mother made sandies, or Mexican wedding cakes, for the church open house, just as she had for twenty years. My father was sequestered in the basement, wrapping gifts on the pool table he had found at the Salvation Army. My parents' arrangement was that my mother did the buying and my father did the wrapping. I broke out my paints and started a new piece, painting with the bedroom door open so that I could feel the warmth from the fireplace and hear The Nutcracker on the stereo. There were cardinals at the bird feeder and popcorn in a large bowl with cranberries to make the chain that went on the tree each year. The house hummed with the festivities of the holiday, and it could have been Little House on the Prairie for how idyllic it was. The world hovered near perfection. For the moment, all was well with the world. Nonetheless, I felt odd. After six months I knew a completely different order of things. I was changed.

"Are things any better with your classmates?" my father asked.

We were walking out in the woods on the watershed. The day was crisp and the sky looked a bit like impending snow, but for the moment it was clear, and we walked under the fir trees along a brook overflowing with ice. My mother and sister were ahead of us, collecting pinecones. I thought about my classmates. I was reasonably sure that they thought I was an idiot. In all likelihood I was driving them crazy with my combination of absurdity and not-so-military demeanor. My decision to brazenly maintain my individuality meant that my choices were often at odds with the requirements of military life. Some of those choices still fill me with regret.

"Is there any kind of issue living with men in the barracks?" my father continued.

My father had some degree of naiveté about the world. He seemed to really think that if the literature said that women were well integrated, then they must be. So the question surprised me a little.

"There are little things," I replied, "the fact that we all live together. You're going to see people in various stages of dress ... or lack thereof."

I thought of the male upperclassman, one more beautifully built than the last, many of them in a barely tied cadet bathrobe or simply a towel as they came out of the latrine after their morning shower. When I caught a glimpse of the perfect forms with cut abdominals and beautiful chests I concluded that God was a sculptor.

And I felt horrendously inadequate in terms of my own physicality.

I brushed a tree branch aside, looked at my father and continued, "For the most part you just ignore those small things. There is an underlying pressure though. It's below the surface, but there is no question that as a woman I feel that I have to prove myself with every task. The pressure comes from the tasks themselves, but it also comes from some of the upperclassmen or even the officers. It depends on the person. Some seem to have no issue at all with women at the Academy. Others just barely tolerate the fact that women are there. It's amazing really that people choose to fight something that is now decided. It's not going to change."

"It takes time," my father mused, "If you think about it, warfare has been almost entirely run by men for thousands of years. Change is difficult. This is a big transition for some people."

But does that excuse it? Does that excuse the fact that the American people pay for our Army and for our Academy, that in a democracy they make the choices about whether our military will be male or female? The Army serves the people it protects. That having been said, there is really no excuse for not embracing the decision of the country and making it work.

This is what one fiercely independent and inexperienced young girl thought about the world. Things were black and white then ... not even just black and white ... but really, really black, and really, really white.

Now, with every birthday I celebrate, the world gets grayer.

My father reached down to pick up a stick lying on the path and tossed it into the brook. The scenery was fabulous, the ice in little cliffs over the water. His stick landed with a cold splash. I could see the thoughts passing across his face.

"I think there is also something to be said about an underlying fear of female soldiers getting wounded ..." he paused, "or dying."

He was looking away, not meeting my eyes. He didn't say what he was thinking... that even though he was thrilled that I was at the Academy, he feared for my safety. This mixture of emotion mirrored my own feelings about West Point ...

several feelings at once. Complicated. Pride and fear simultaneously.

Women coming home dead.

I thought about that for a minute, about the smell of dirt and grime mixed with M16 shells on a firing range where the targets are shaped like people. You couldn't get away from the bottom-line purpose of the Academy. For all of the fanfare, for all of the days where the Corps marched out on the Plain looking like beautiful tin soldiers, they were training to "close with (the enemy) by means of fire and maneuver"[20] and destroy him. This was training for war. There was no getting around it.

At eighteen it never occurred to me that I could be among the dead.

About three days before the end of leave, I began to dread my return to West Point. The hours dwindled quickly and before I knew it, my father and I stood once again at that same spot outside Grant Hall. There was a little snow on the ground and it clung to the edges of my father's loafers as he walked around the car to say goodbye.

He held me tightly.

"Now you can do this, okay?" he said. "Don't doubt yourself."

I nodded against the puff of his coat with determination, biting back tears. The military required no "P.D.A.," or public display of affection, so the hug was brief.

I took my bag, with the little Tupperware that my mother had packed with a sandwich and Christmas cookies, and started toward the cadet area. Looking back once, I saw him standing by the car. In that instant I longed to be a little girl again, on my father's lap, safe, secure, wanting nothing.

I can still see him in the twilight, looking after me, sending in his gaze all of his heart and will, luck and strength. As I looked back he simply raised his hand as he always did, a ges-

---

[20] Part of the mission of the Infantry.

ture that said, "Go get 'em, kid." And with no alternative but to turn into the fray, I memorized the image. Tucking it away, I turned and pinged into the company area to begin it all again.

I stood on the scale in the sinks the next morning. I weighed 147 pounds.

10

I came around the corner of Grant Hall and was swept up in the motion of the Corps. Christmas Leave was a distant memory in under sixty seconds. With cadets moving smartly in every direction, the Areas and buildings were covered with dozens of grey "ants" moving with a purpose. West Point had its own life force, its own pulse. With my bag in tow, I "fell in," my free arm dropping straight and my feet picking up an accelerated pace, nearly of their own accord, assuming the stature of a fourth class cadet.

The first order of business was to find the semester's room assignments. Moments later, bag still in tow, I stood at the position of attention in front of the company bulletin board. It was amazing how one small sheet of paper could mean glee or misery for a cadet. The good news was that my roommate was to be Lisa Mayer, a girl with whom I was reasonably friendly.

The next piece of news, however, was not so good. Lisa and I were assigned to a room at the top of the stairs on the third floor, which meant pinging up two flights of stairs with all of my crap. I inwardly groaned. If I had had the guts to fall out in the middle of the hallway I would have stamped my foot, wagged my head and displayed my disappointment, but as is required with plebe life, all emotions are kept locked inside, and for once, nothing showed on my face.

As if the room location were not enough, the real news of the day was headlined on the chain of command chart, which was posted to the side of the room list. I leaned between two of my classmates to peek at it, all the while at the position of attention. Sure enough, there his name was, Cadet Bailey, and

God help me, he was my new squad leader. I didn't know whether to be thrilled or terrified.

How Matt Bailey ended up my squad leader for second semester, plebe year is a mystery to me. Did he volunteer? Or was it simply luck of the draw?

As I stood in front of the bulletin board, the sound of low quarters on the floor of the barracks, the smell of sweaty wool trousers already filling the hallway, my feelings were layered and complex. Maybe a little glee? I'd get to see the object of my affection every day. But that could be overkill. There it was, sneaking up behind me ... a completely different emotion ... maybe a little dread? Cadet Bailey was high speed in a way that I watched in awe from a distance, not really even grasping. It seemed unlikely that I could live up to his standards. This could be a nightmare beyond the bounds of imagination.

"This will probably be a great new experience," said my father.

"Uh huh," I said loudly on the pay phone in the basement later that night, trying to sound optimistic. As usual, there were cadets outside the door doing pushups and I could hardly hear my father for the "whooahs."

"Think of all you can learn," he continued cheerfully.

"Five more! Five more!" the voice outside the payphone called.

"Yes, of course," I replying, raising my voice to be heard over the noise.

"Focus on the positive," he said.

I rolled my eyes. God love him, he always saw the most treacherous parts of life's journey as a learning experience. Meanwhile, he could never imagine just how much hell one upperclassman could create.

Two hours later the Corps gathered for accountability formation and my new roommate and I stood in our new spots in Cadet Bailey's squad on the Area. It was cold and we shivered while we stood in our short overcoats. In the two minutes before the command to Fall In, the doors to the stoops swung open and crashed repeatedly as the upperclassmen came to formation, their low quarters clicking against the steps. They chatted with each other on the latest news while all of the plebes looked straight ahead as they stood at attention with their backs to the barracks. I stood with my eyes unwavering under my grey hat, hoping that the upperclassmen might leave us alone at least until the next day.

The Corps fell in.

"Company, Attennnntion," called the new first sergeant, with the lilt on the last syllable.

Depression covered me like a blanket. I already missed my family and the semester stretched like a marathon in front of me, a sea of countless and unknown challenges and frustrations ahead. As always, I longed for the safety I felt when I was curled up under the covers in my own bed at home where everyone was nice and kind, and I was loved.

The knock on the door came twice, the signal of an upperclassman knocking, and I instinctively knew it was him.

BAM! BAM!

Lisa and I rose immediately to our feet.

"ENTER SIR," we called in unison.

He walked into the room and I stood at the position of attention dutifully like any plebe when her squad leader bestows a visit. Cadet Bailey was still in his dress grey, looking like the strack, squared away former first sergeant that he was. His uniform lay across his chest without a wrinkle, and his hat perched square on his head. His shoes were edge dressed and spit shined. He was the epitome of cadet perfection and he embodied everything that seemed far out of reach for me.

A bit of hero worship began to take hold.

Meanwhile, I was looking less than strack. I had been sweeping the floor and now was holding the broom awkwardly, not sure whether I should not move at all or put it down. Cadet Bailey didn't pay any attention. I couldn't help noticing how his hat sat on his head as if it dared not move.

"Beaudean, Mayer, how are things going?" he asked.

"Fine Sir," we said in unison.

Fine? Our room, in disorganized piles around us, was a testament to the fact that things were in complete disorder. I had caught a glimpse of Matt Bailey's room through his open doorway on the way up the stairs, and sure enough, his bed was neatly made and uniforms put away. Meanwhile, we were a train wreck.

He looked around the room at the disarray.

"I think you have some distance to go tonight," he mused, "because you'll need to be ready for AMI[21] tomorrow morning."

I nodded, my head bobbing up and down with the broom in my hand, some sad plebe bobble head doll.

He looked at me thoughtfully over the pile of underwear at my feet.

"Don't nod at me Beaudean," he said quietly, "just go back to your four responses."

"Yes Sir," I replied dutifully.

Good grief. I was surprised that Matt Bailey didn't take me by the arm, walk me to the edge of the Cadet Area and say, "Beaudean, don't come back."

"The key with the room," he went on without missing a beat, "is to make your bed first. Make your bed and the room instantly looks better. You two have a lot of ground to cover this evening and I expect you to be ready tomorrow morning. I'll be by each morning to take a look at your room. In addition, we'll meet every morning outside my room at 0550 hours to go over the training schedule for the day, your knowledge and your uniform. Is that understood?"

"Yes Sir," we replied in unison and with requisite enthusiasm.

---

[21] Morning room inspection.

I inwardly groaned. What *was* it with these people and these inhumanly early hours?

Lisa and I were up until two that night, lights off, door open to provide hallway light as we folded our uniforms and readied the room for morning inspection.

Lisa was a tall girl with a brown bob of hair and freckles on her nose. She had been recruited by the Academy to play varsity softball, but she struggled academically. Lisa had a terrific personality, a mix of good humor and the ability to strike a friendship with nearly anyone. She was also fiercely loyal. Most important to me, she struggled with her weight just as I did. Our room would have no boodle box as we began to partner in the quest for thinness. By two a.m. I arrived at the conclusion that I had found, like I had with my Beast roommate, someone to share in the agony. As we said goodnight, I sat up on my elbow to survey the room. Cadet Bailey was right. The room looked infinitely better once the beds were made. I had a funny feeling that Cadet Bailey would be right in general.

To this day, the first thing I always do when cleaning or organizing the house is to make the bed.

The next morning, my new roommate and I stood tall on the wall just outside of Cadet Bailey's room. My roommate executed a right face and knocked three times on the door.

"Beaudean, how many days until Graduation?" His voice called from inside the room and in a whoosh of air the door swung open, the trash can bounced from his foot loudly to the edge of the door, holding it open ninety degrees and he poked his head out, already neatly attired in As-for-class, his tie wrapped in a perfect knot.

"Sir," I started, but faltered. The whole scene had me off guard.

Because ....

Unfortunately I had not been thinking about the Days as Lisa and I left our room and pinged down the stairs to land outside of Matt Bailey's room. Instead of going over the Days and the New York Times in my mind, focusing, readying myself for the morning's queries, there I was ... yes, I admit it.... fantasizing about Matt Bailey in various versions of Dress Grey.

There is a field of wildflowers and I am wearing a beautiful dress, very Vogue, looking thin and fabulous, a chic and sexy version of myself reeking of class, a version that Anna Wintour would be proud of. There he is up ahead, looking the knight that he is ... we rush across the field to meet each other. Sunshine washes across the daisies. Hallelujahs are sung. The angels weep. He kisses me madly, we're sinking into the grass ...

"Beaudean!" Now the voice was uncomfortably sharp.

Matt Bailey meant business. With no interest in my good humor, perfect teeth, and magnetic smile, he was focused on one thing, bringing his not-so-squared-away-and-even-a-bit-rebellious plebe in line.

All of this flashed through my mind in about three seconds as I stood with my back to Cadet Bailey's wall with his voice bellowing out of the doorway. And that little bit of adrenaline that gets saved for moments for which we are not prepared came running through my bloodstream.

"Beaudean! I think maybe this morning's knowledge has escaped you already."

"No Sir," I replied with the barest whisper of edge just beneath my voice.

Those who knew me recognized the suggestion of rebellion just below the surface and Cadet Bailey would soon come to know the barely audible lilt. He would soon recognize my rebellious nature and it would become the heart of our unspoken battle.

The morning's recitation was reasonably acceptable, but Cadet Bailey accepted nothing less than excellence.

"Go down to formation you two," he said, as the minute caller came out to take his place, "and let's try it again tomorrow at 0540 hours, just to make sure we have enough time."

The next morning Lisa and I arrived on cue at 0540 hours on the dot. This time I was ready. Thoroughly ready. And with succinct military exactness, I popped off every piece of memorization that Matt Bailey could conjure up.

"Good job Beaudean," he said, looking up from polishing one of his low quarters, "We're back to 0550 hours tomorrow."

"Yes Sir," I replied. He wouldn't best me. If he thought he could rule me, he was sadly mistaken.

And so it began.

Each morning Lisa and I reported to Cadet Bailey's room. We knocked, and Bailey would swing open the door, he and his very hot roommate in various stages of dress, working on cleaning their room, which often smelled of farts and maleness. I sometimes wondered as I fought the urge to wrinkle my nose that my admiration for Cadet Bailey was misplaced. What I was to learn over the course of the semester was that he was a man's man – a hunter, fisherman, a true blue, red-blooded American male. And he was whooah to the max. Sometimes we would knock on his door at 0550 hours and his roommate would open it. There Cadet Bailey would be, doing pushups at the crack of dawn. At moments like this I was amazed at his early morning motivation and simultaneously wondered whether this level of commitment was really required for good military leadership. On many a day I wished that he would just relax.

I quickly learned that Bailey's morning quizzes were not to be taken lightly. He drilled us on our knowledge with a tenacity that never seemed to quell. In addition, I thought I detected in him a desire to rule me, to break my spirit. This is where he underestimated me. It was an unspoken battle of wills, but a battle nonetheless.

In a way, Bailey was cleverer than perhaps he even knew. By trying to break me of my individuality, he prodded me to fight hard to master each task, if only to thwart him and win each day's battle for dominion. I studied the newspaper, memorized The Days, and studied newly assigned knowledge on the various branches of the Army. Despite the new resolve, I carved out in my own mind and my own will a place for myself and my own thoughts. Besides, I was a quick study when it came to memorization, and I mastered the knowledge for each day and then went back to my own thoughts deep inside, disappearing into my own imagination.

There was no question, however, that Cadet Bailey brought out the best in me. Even with my continued foibles and inadequacy, I was the best cadet I had been to date. Despite the occasional spill at breakfast, my uniform looked sharp, I knew my knowledge and I completed my duties. He seemed reasonably satisfied.

At every turn, my strong performance satisfied his high standards, but I took a small pleasure in the tiny remnants of my person that I exhibited in full view and with no apology. My copy of *Harpers Bazaar* and *Vogue* were visible in the desk drawer during AMI inspection, the lacy underwear peeked out while he inspected my foot locker, the defiant look in my eyes took over when I had had enough nonsense for one day.

The days were beginning to grow longer and the mood of the Corps lifted with the thaw. The fourth class was looking forward to Recognition Day, which was only two months away, the firsties hungrily anticipating their Graduation Day. As I chatted with Lisa during study hours, we were joined by several of her friends and propped the door open the 90 degrees required when male and female cadets were in a barracks room together.

We were all laughing and sharing a soda, with Lisa's friend regaling us with the story of his midnight run to spin the spurs of Thayer's Statue[22] in the hope for better luck on an exam. We howled with mirth, and at a particularly funny section, I put my head back and laughed with abandon. As I turned my head, I saw him come to the top of the stairs, watching me as I laughed.

"Yes, you'll control my performance, but this is my soul, and you'll never have it," I thought to myself, willing the words to make their way to him. Oddly, I sensed that he understood where I drew the line in the sand.

Because my performance was acceptable, our morning sessions grew more conversational in nature. Truth was, Cadet Bailey was a fascinating human being. There was something about him that attracted me in a way I couldn't even put my finger on. Maybe it was because military life seemed to come so easily to him, while I was such a fish out of water. For Cadet Bailey, cadet life was a natural fit. He was born to lead and looked the part. He *was* the part.

By April, graduation for the first class and "Recognition" for plebes were right around the corner. My classmates and I would be "recognized" and would no longer address the upperclass cadets as Sir or Ma'am. Plebe year, for all of its agony, would be complete.

We all counted the days.

Cadet Bailey opted to try for Ranger School during the coming summer. Only the most athletic and military minded had any chance of making it through the school in the nine weeks allotted for cadet leave. He included us in his training regimen and the entire squad took a study break at 2100 hours each night for pushups and sit-ups. Cadet Bailey also added pull-ups to the mix, of which I could not do one.

---

[22] West Point lore includes the legend that cadets who pilgrimage to the statue of Sylvanus Thayer to spin his spurs are guaranteed luck on an exam.

"Okay, now Beaudean, plant yourself on the bar, focus on pulling from the back," he said as we stood in the sinks one evening.

"Right, *plant* myself," I thought a little sarcastically. But I said nothing and attempted to convey enthusiasm.

Cadet Bailey stood behind me as I hung from the miserable pull-up bar, ready to humiliate myself.

"Okay, whenever you're ready," he said.

I pulled for dear life to get my chin up above the metal pole.

"All you, all you," he said as he basically boosted my ass up so that I could reach the bar. What a laugh. It was truly "all him" doing the lifting. To his credit, he never criticized my athletic prowess or lack thereof and nearly always encouraged.

As he spotted me on the pull-up, I prayed that by some miracle he wouldn't notice the cellulite on my thighs. As he grabbed my hips I cringed. It was one small nightly event, but it fed my sense of unacceptability and ugliness. The seeds that were being planted, one here, one there, gathered momentum on the pull-up bar.

I came off the bar and he let go of my hips.

"Good job Beaudean," he said.

Could I read his thoughts? Was he thinking, as I did, that if I weighed less, I might have some chance of doing the pull-up myself? I pinged up the stairs. The hallway was unusually quiet and I took a moment to stand at the position of attention in front of the full-length mirror. Something had to be done.

I weighed 147 pounds.

Around the same time, the class of 1989 celebrated 500th Night, when the cows celebrated 500 days until their own graduation. It was a big to-do. The evening included a formal dinner and dance and most of the young men flew in their girlfriends for the evening. Cadet Bailey was no different.

I dropped off the last bundle of laundry for the day and pinged over to visit Jill. Lisa was there already, as was Jill's roommate, and we all gathered around the window for "dress watching," during which we critiqued the dresses of the civilian dates who paraded through the Area over the course of the evening.

I had eyes for only one couple. I watched from the window as she stood with him on the stoops. Formal events, like Homecoming Weekend, were one time where civilians were allowed in the Cadet Area. It was odd to see colors other than grey out in the spots where we normally stood.

Cadet Bailey's girlfriend was lovely. Her dress was long and pink, her hair in long, curled strands. She carried a small pink purse and stood in high heels while she and Bailey chatted with his friends. As if there were not enough about which to be jealous, Cadet Bailey's girlfriend was thin. *Really thin.* And as with so many small and seemingly insignificant events, I equated her beauty with her size, and felt that it simply might never be possible for me to be anything that a man like Cadet Bailey might pursue.

"If I were thinner, maybe I'd have a chance," I thought to myself.

Who would want me as I was?

There was no question about it. Thinner was better, any way you looked at it. I said goodnight to my friends and despite the early evening hour, got into my pajamas and into bed. There was only one place that felt safe and comforting and it was beneath the covers where the world around me disappeared, even if only for a few hours. The room darkened in the twilight and I stayed there huddled under the covers, hating myself and my own body, wishing I could be perfect, thin and beautiful.

147 pounds.

11

I swear Beaudean, I don't know how you concentrate with that much activity on your desk. I have to keep it simple."

Cadet Bailey was looking down at the blotter on my desk. His own desk barely had the three knickknacks that cadets were allowed. It was devoid of distraction. Very military. Mine was decorated with pictures, colorful and cartoon-like, with each completed day marked out in green.

"So how are things going with your weight?" he asked, switching topics.

It was late April. The annual physical fitness test, the APFT,[23] was just three weeks away. The inference was clear. Thinner equaled faster equaled better.

There was a pause.

"Fine Sir," I replied, "I've been working out more."

This was the only acceptable response.

The truth was that I was failing. I knew that I had gained fifteen pounds since R Day and that I was discussed and even laughed at by my company mates. To avoid their criticism, I never took food back to my room from the Mess Hall, conscious of even the appearance that I was snacking. But I began to sneak food, buying it from Boodlers, the snack bar inside the cadet area, which was accessible during the evening hours. I'd hurry up the stairs to Boodlers after dark, looking furtively about like a thief. Praying that no one would see, I would race inside, grab a pint of ice cream, pay quickly and tear out of the place. Food was my comfort on a bad day. It was my reward on a good day. All the while I wished that I

---

[23] The Army's physical fitness test (sometimes called the APRT). Cadets must perform as many pushups and situps as possible in two minutes and complete a two mile run for time.

could magically wake up one morning and look like my new friend, Katherine McNeil.

Katherine McNeil, or "Kat," as we called her, came from a life completely different from my own. She was the daughter of a West Point grad and her sister graduated from the Academy as well. While a good student and athlete in high school, there was no question that Kat's claim to fame was instead her popularity, magnetic personality and ribald sense of humor. She was also a knock-out and practically stepped off the pages of *Vogue* – a long, willowy blond with an hourglass figure. Kat was the homecoming queen and owned a red convertible. I had seen the pictures. The car completed the picture of the beautiful young blond with her following of would-be suitors.

While it was hard not to be envious, it was equally hard not to like Kat. She had a fun personality and terrific sense of humor. And despite her thin form, she shared with Lisa and me the battle to be as thin as humanly possible -- the never-ending effort to make the uniform look good.

The room was dark as Lisa gently shook my shoulder to wake me and with eyes barely open, I swung my legs over the side of the bed. Without uttering a word we both pulled on our Army sweatpants and sneakers. It was 0515 hours and the barracks were quiet. Despite the fact that no one was awake, we pinged out the door and down the stairs, squaring corners as we went.

A good cadet didn't just follow the rules when someone was watching.

Within minutes we were standing in the sinks.

I stepped on the scale hoping that by some miracle I would have grown three inches and dropped fifteen pounds.

148 … again.

A door opened and Kat emerged, attired in identical sweats. Without a word, we mounted the stairs from the basement to the Area and trotted out to the end of the cadet area, breaking into a run as we went.

Determined to be thin, I started each day with next to nothing for breakfast. By the fourth hour of class my blood sugar was low and my hands were shaking. Hunger took over and I looked for the closest source of snack food, desperate to eat the first thing I got my hands on. At lunch, I'd eat again. In the afternoon I would run, promising myself that I'd burn enough calories to counteract the morning binge. But a three-mile run only burns about 300 calories and could never make up for the amount of food I was taking in. After the run, I was hungry again. I would eat dinner. On many evenings I would promise myself that tomorrow would be different and still make my evening run to Boodlers. I would go to bed loathing myself and wake the next morning to begin the cycle again.

We all shared in the daily pursuit of the "perfect" body. We constantly discussed how to stay thin, how to eat less in the Mess Hall, how to burn more calories in our workouts. I soon noticed that female cadets across the Corps struggled with us, all in a silent understanding that to be a "fat female cadet" was the worst fate possible. And there were all sorts of different coping mechanisms. I knew a girl on the women's track team who used to eat a "salad sandwich" for lunch – two pieces of bread with salad in the middle. Lisa worked out with her softball team. As for Kat, she rarely ate at night, and then usually only air puffed popcorn. It was a consciousness that resonated with most if not all female cadets, a common call to somehow just lose a few more.

If only I were thin, I'd be okay ... I'd be acceptable.
148 1/2 pounds.

The night before we were to be recognized I stood in formation in my usual spot. I had come to recognize the sound of Cadet Bailey's step, the rhythm of his footfall on the stone steps. He was still buttoning his short overcoat when he came to stand in front of me.

"What's the news Beaudean?" he asked while examining the bottom buttonhole before putting it in place over its respective brass button. Lisa was still at softball practice. I had him all to myself.

On evenings like this we exchanged philosophical ideas about leadership or chatted about current events. His view of the world was different than mine but his philosophy was as well-reasoned as my own and I learned a great deal from our conversations. I think he had come to care about me. I was becoming more disciplined. I wanted to believe that he saw in me the potential for good leadership.

In answer to his question about the news, I was well prepared and began my recitation.

"Sir," I began, "today in the New York Times, it was reported that ..."

"No, no, stop," he interrupted. Our eyes met and I could have sworn, as I had felt so many times before, that there was something there besides the care of a squad leader for his plebe, more than just a professional relationship. The warmth rushed to my face.

"No," he said, "not the paper. How did your day go? Anything new?"

For a moment I was speechless. He had never been so familiar with me before.

"Well Sir, tomorrow is recognition," I said happily.

"Yes, it is," he answered, his face widening into a smile that matched mine.

At that moment, with his face glowing with warmth, I thought he was the handsomest man I had ever seen.

Years later it would occur to me that Cadet Bailey was much like my father. He had that same drive for perfection, unwavering standards and a moral compass that made him an admirable human being, respected by many, just like my dad. While not the best looking fellow in the room, it was the way he conducted himself that made him attractive. Like my father, my squad leader watched me struggle, allowed me to fail even, but was firmly behind me with his encouragement. The two men were also equally impossible to satisfy. No matter how great my latest accomplishment, there was always another hurdle.

"How's it going with your weight?" my father would ask every so often during an evening phone call.

My heart would sink.

The well intentioned persistence and drive of the two most influential men in my life, combined with my growing hatred of my body was helping to shape a sinister new character in my life.

The day of the Recognition Parade, the most important day in a fourth classman's life, I was a miserable 150 pounds. The tremendous accomplishment of the day was diminished by that number. As we marched off the Plain and back to the barracks the upper classmen lined up to shake our hands to congratulate us on the completion of plebe year. It should have felt like a victory. Instead, I shook Cadet Bailey's hand knowing that I would never measure up to his standards. Recognition Day, long awaited and anticipated, with the preceding days meticulously crossed off with green marker, came and went. No achievement could possibly make up for the fact that I was fat.

"I think it has something to do with the distributor."

It was my father's voice. He was in the front yard, outside my window. I could hear him talking with my mother. The white curtains of my bedroom swayed gently to the sound of my father tinkering with the lawnmower. There were no raised voices, no din in the hallway, no smell of sweaty trousers, no cadets lining up in shining fanfare for an afternoon parade on the Plain. The world had not ended. I was still myself. My life was still intact. My family was in place, unharmed, oblivious to the machinations of the US Army. I was thankful to be home.

I rose to my knees on the bed and pushing the curtains aside, looked out the window at my father.

"Hey," I called.

He turned from where he was cursing at the lawnmower and his face broke into a wide smile.

"Hey there kid, how was your first night of freedom?"

"Great," I replied with a grin, "Hang on. I'll come out and help you."

We stood side by side in the yard, looking identical with our hands on our hips, peering down at the engine, both of us clueless as to why it wouldn't start. I didn't care. I was happy. I had his love.

Little had changed in the year I had been gone. There was a garden to weed, vegetables to harvest, jam to be made, summer cookouts to be planned. Church was promptly at nine on Sunday mornings and my family sat together in the front pew on the right, as we always had. It was as if I had never left. West Point was far away.

Friends queried me about every detail of my existence in cadet grey -- fascinated, probing. Initially the questions were superficial. Was it tough? Had it been what I expected? They were so proud of me, blah, blah, blah. The most common question? "What is it like to be a woman at West Point?" And what they were really asking -- Was there sexual harassment? Was there inappropriateness? Was there sex in the barracks? The focus was inevitably on the male to female ratio of ten to one where each male body is more beautiful than the last.

My answers were vague and mixed. West Point isn't a simple experience to define. Nor was it simple to define what it was like to be a woman in such a place.

The two week break disappeared like a speeding train. Just about the time I caught up on my sleep, it was time to hit the ground running again. The yearlings[24] were due back for accountability formation at 1800 hours and, before I knew it, I was standing tall in my white over grey with the rest of my classmates.

---

[24] Second year cadet, also called a "yuck."

The yearling class would spend the summer training at a location about ten miles from West Point proper. Camp Buckner had been an Academy institution for decades and was Part II of Army military field training. The summer was dedicated to learning about how the branches of the Army functioned in synchronicity. It was also eight weeks of feeling dirty, hot and sweaty.

Not my favorite.

The itinerary was packed. We would learn about the Corps of Engineers and how the Corps built bridges, structures and roads. We would construct the Bailey Bridge, my platoon working as a team to heave the enormous bridge components into place. The summer training included an introduction to Armor. We would fly to Fort Knox to learn about tanks and armored personnel carriers. We would learn about the Field Artillery and how it supports the forces on the front lines, loading 100 pound rounds into a howitzer. There would be classes on the M60 machine gun, Claymore mines, grenades, how to clear a minefield and land navigation. There were obstacle courses and hand-to-hand combat, bayonet fighting and survival skills. During Infantry Week we would learn the basics of patrolling, formed in a V-shaped formation with one of us "on point." We would search the woods for the enemy at three in the morning, the black sky occasionally lit up by flares sent up by the OpFor.[25]

My class was "shuffled" for the summer, organized into eight companies with a completely different set of classmates to train with. Each platoon slept in a metal barracks with a small room in the corner for the girls. Each day started with P.T. followed by field training. Some of the classes were interesting, but for the most part I was hot, sweaty and weighed 151 pounds, and I was sure my platoon mates saw me as dead weight. Listening to the rain pound on the corrugated metal

---

[25] During various field exercises the part of the enemy was played by the Opposition Forces, who were usually military personnel tasked specifically with acting the part of "Charlie," or the enemy, during our training operations.

roof of the barracks one night, I concluded that essentially Camp Buckner was one step up from sleeping outside.

One day … One day I'll have room service.

Camp Buckner was an education in how the Army worked as a whole. But there was another piece of education as well. That summer also introduced me to the idea that while men could be wonderful teammates, they could also be chauvinistic and disgusting.

"What was that like, living in such close quarters?"

My friend and I were having coffee at Pershing Square, the breakfast nook across from Grand Central Station in New York City. It was fifteen years after my summer at Camp Buckner, and here I was once again answering the question, "What was it like to be a woman at West Point?"

"Did you really drive a tank?" she continued.

I laughed.

"Yes, once," I replied and then said knowingly, "If you're asking what I think you're asking, you want to know what it was like living in such close proximity with men."

She smiled and nodded.

I thought a minute and took a bite of waffle before continuing.

"There was one afternoon during the second summer, at Camp Buckner. My squad was riding in the back of a 5-ton truck back to the barracks. One of the guys had a porn magazine and started reading an article out loud. Before I knew it, the conversation escalated and the comments turned vile, just about who had done what sexually, etc., etc. Really graphic. Frankly, with my limited experience, some of the terminology was new to me! But I knew that it was denigrating to women. I was completely disgusted, but I didn't say anything. I sat there in the back of that truck and put up with it, all the while feeling completely demoralized."

"You didn't say anything?" my friend asked, horrified, "Why not?!"

I thought back to that day. How do you explain to a civilian that when you are living in the woods with a bunch of guys playing Army and women are the 10% minority, you don't want to be perceived as anything but a team player?

"To say something or report him was unthinkable," I replied, taking a sip of coffee, "It never occurred to me to take action. As a female cadet who was struggling to keep up with the guys, the last thing I wanted to do was alienate myself further by creating a stink. I was nineteen years old, immature, willing to do anything to be accepted."

I tapered off, shaking my head as I remembered the scene, the engine of the truck roaring and my classmate reading that disgusting article.

"Tell ya what though," I continued, giving my friend a long look, "Now, at thirty five, I'm not afraid of being called the bitch anymore. If I had known then what I know now, I would have reported his ass in a heartbeat and made his life a living hell."

With five weeks of Camp Buckner complete, my parents came up for a visit on a Sunday afternoon. My mother brought a picnic lunch for us complete with egg salad sandwiches and, of course, a pie.

The world, after all, could be made better with pie.

My mother looked at me thoughtfully as I conveyed the latest in our training, the occasional sexual harassment and my own lack of talent.

"Sometimes I keep up P.T. and it feels like the biggest win," I said, "Then other days, I don't do very well. My legs aren't fast enough and I can't keep up."

My mother was quiet. She was thinking of our history.

"You come from a long line of strong women," she said, looking at me across the picnic blanket.

I nodded. I knew.

The Byrne family came from Ireland in the early 1900s, a large family with five daughters and one son, my grandfather.

Soon after arriving in America, my great grandfather walked out on Grandma Carrie and the children, who were all under the age of eighteen. They called a family meeting and determined that they would work together to support the family. My grandfather and one sister were young, so they stayed in school. The other four sisters went to work in New York City, starting out as seamstresses and cooks, educating themselves so that they could gain better employment as secretaries or assistants. Through their sheer grit and will, all moved on to successful careers as businesswomen in Manhattan.

"So you come from a long line of strong women," my mother concluded.

She never doubted me for a moment. My mother shared with me years later that she sometimes felt sorry for West Point.

"As strong and fierce as the Army is, they've never seen someone like you."

She took my hand and squeezed it, and then, taking a piece of string out of the lunch basket, where it had tied up the deli meats, she cut off a piece and tied it around my finger to make a little ring. She looked at me, the daughter she adored, the daughter she believed the Army didn't deserve.

"Each minute of each day here, you remember who you are. You remember the strength that you come from. The women who came before you built *extraordinary* lives. You come from that blood. The Army will never break you, because you won't allow it. When you look at this string, you think of that."

I looked down at the little ring of string on my finger. For the next three weeks, I never fell out of another run and I didn't shed another tear.

Days later I stood under the water in the female shower. After a hot day of training with dirt, sawdust and sweat in every crevice of my body, I reveled in the water. Ahhh, to be clean. With five weeks of Camp Buckner completed, I felt a tremendous sense of accomplishment. The water ran over me and I looked down at the little string tied around my finger. It was filthy and I took it off my finger and carefully washed the little loop of rope, and then added it to the chain around my neck so that it rested on top of my dogtags. There it would stay, a reminder of the long line of strong women, my mother's love and her unshakeable belief in my strength and resolve.

151 pounds.

12

"Don't say a fucking word," grunted Mike Miller as he picked up his gear.

Mike, my "ranger buddy," was a living, breathing G.I. Joe doll.

And he had a rock hard set of abs that matched his stubborn head.

I knew I probably wasn't Mike's first choice for ranger buddy, but I thought it made sense to work together. My initial strategy had been to make friends. But Mike had no interest in any girl in the middle of *his* field training and no amount of friendliness would undo his disgust. For six weeks I followed Mike from training task to training task, generally straining to keep up while my buddy set a blistering pace and rolled his eyes, cursing profusely at my lack of athletic ability and military prowess.

There was some justice, however, for while Mike Miller mastered nearly every task with alacrity, he was a lousy shot. On the day that I qualified with my M-16 with a near perfect thirty eight rounds out of forty, Mike failed the test not once but twice. While the rest of the platoon marched on to the next training area, like a good ranger buddy, I waited for him to attempt the firing range for the third time.

Apparently three was a charm.

"Just don't say a fucking word," he said again as he gathered his gear.

I said nothing, but smiled to myself and silently enjoyed watching the oh-so-military Mike Miller struggle to pass basic rifle marksmanship. We struck out together for the next training site, Mike's long legs setting the pace while I scrambled to keep up with his quick stride. The next training area was two clicks[26] away but with Mike's blistering pace we would make it in under 25 minutes.

"I've gotta pee," I said, panting.

"Mother fucker Beaudean," he groaned. He always called me by my last name. *What an ass.*

Without another word and certainly no apology, I walked into the woods, found a tree to duck behind and began the elaborate process reserved for female soldiers, the process of undoing and unloading all the straps and equipment and gear so that the trousers could be dropped to squat.

"I swear to God, if I had a nickel for every minute of the day you have to take a piss," called Mike.

"Yeah, well, if I had a nickel for every minute you were an asshole," I yelled back from behind the tree. I was now working to get all my gear back on.

"Wish ya had a dick don't cha Beaudean?" Mike called.

"Up yours," I yelled back.

"Y'know, if we were on patrol and Charlie was running around these woods, they'd wait for us to be apart just like this and then pick us off. You'd barely have time to raise your rifle," he called.

"Well, at least when I take aim, I'll hit the guy, unlike you, who can't hit the side of a barn," I yelled back.

"Y'know, fuck you Beaudean," he was pissed now.

"Right back atcha asshole," I yelled back, undaunted.

It was a match made in heaven.

The art of war has a complexity I had never imagined. Every single task, every weapon, every technique was new to me. I was fascinated. I listened intently as an NCO instructor explained the process for changing an M60 machine gun barrel. Who knew that the barrel of a machine gun could grow so hot that the metal softened and it had to be changed? Or that razor wire obstacles could be cut with an explosive device called a bangalore torpedo? Or that there were so many types

---

[26] Kilometer.

of hand grenades? Incendiary. Frag. Colored smoke. The Army had apparently thought of one for every scenario. I had to admit, it was mighty clever.

I knew that war meant destruction, but I was still surprised at the noise and devastation. The engines of the tanks were loud. The guns were deafening. With every grenade thrown and every mortar round lobbed onto a hillside far away, I hated the decimation but was amazed at the power. There was no question that summer as the rounds hit their marks and the soldiers demonstrated their skills -- this was the best Army the world had ever known.

Despite the daily focus on all that was "whooah," I refused to relinquish the feminine side of my life. I carried a toothbrush in my ammunition pouch and when no one was looking, brushed my teeth with a little paste and water from my canteen just to feel clean and refreshed. My toenails were neatly painted underneath my OD green socks. *Vogue* magazine was stashed under the pile of tactical equipment in my foot locker. Despite the greasy camouflage paint we wore on our faces, I wore mascara every day. It made me feel human. Underneath the uniform, I was still a young woman. With every show of femininity, Mike hated me more. When I weighed in that summer at 153, I sealed my fate as the fat female yearling who didn't fit in.

Mike and I made good time despite my bathroom break. Jogging along with our gear, we arrived in time to join the group assembled in front of eight Special Forces instructors.

Time for hand-to-hand combat and bayonet training.

The "rubber ducks," black rubber versions of the M16 with affixed bayonet, were heavy, heavier than the actual rifle. Despite the black leather gloves protecting my hands, my fingers were soon blistered as I learned to wield the bayonet to strike the enemy. We learned to swipe and thrust the rifle with its bayonet to stab our opponent, or slash his face, to use the butt to crush his head. There is no distant, anonymous way to take the enemy's life in close quarters combat.

This is the sort of contact where one can see the eyes of the enemy and the sweat on their brow.

"Whadaya think Beaudean," Mike yelled from the next row of cadets, "D'ya think you can take Charlie when he overruns the perimeter?"

I was panting with exertion. My shoulders were rolled forward with the weight of the rubber duck, which hung on my hands.

"Cause if you don't take him he just might take you," he taunted, "You know what happens to female prisoners of war, right?"

I looked at my Ranger buddy and wondered if the name of the enemy was Charlie or Mike.

"See, if you had done your job in the first place and actually *hit* the enemy with that rifle of yours, he wouldn't be overrunning our position. Y'know, the M16 isn't just for decoration," I called back.

There were chuckles nearby.

"Fuck off," was Mike's reply, but I had won this round.

I suspected that the three days of hand-to-hand combat training would not end without some sort of test to measure our skills. On the last day as we stood around the ring made of hay bales and full of sawdust, my heart began to sink.

"Cadets, you'll now put on protective gear," yelled the instructor, "and practice your skills against an opponent selected by us."

I looked at the pile of helmets, chest protectors and groin cups at his feet.

I barely heard the instructor's commentary about the grading process and how one opponent could defeat the other. I looked around at my classmates -- the taut bodies honed through training and weight lifting -- and wondered just how bruised I'd be by the end of the afternoon.

The first two yearlings stepped into the ring, clad with chest pads, a helmet, a mouth protector, groin cup, knee pads and elbow pads. The fighting quickly commenced and I watched as the two young men in the ring used the pugel sticks to beat the living crap out of each other. The trainers called the match and a winner. The next two contenders stepped into the hay bale circle. As they readied themselves to duke it out, my mind wandered back to an earlier day, when my weapon had not been a pugel stick, but something far more basic.

The bane of my existence in the fourth grade was Jeff Russo. Jeff was a big kid for his age and carried a briefcase to school. We shared the same route to the bus stop and it quickly became obvious that he had a schoolyard crush. As he tried to hold my hand, I pulled away in disgust. When his overtures didn't work, Jeff became angry and the daily walk to the bus stop became its own version of hell, with my suitor throwing stones at me, taunting me and generally making my life miserable.

As I relayed the circumstances to my parents, my mother encouraged me to take the high ground, to ignore him, to leave for the bus early, to negotiate. My father, despite what doubts he may have harbored, allied with my mother. Dinner each night began with a "Jeff Russo update" and I wearily relayed Jeff's latest antics while my parents made suggestions as to how to deal with the situation in a mature, peaceful fashion.

Initially I agreed with my mother that the best route to resolution was to find a diplomatic solution, but as the months passed and the harassment grew more pronounced, nothing seemed to work.

On a rainy day in late March the situation came to a head. Jeff traded in pebbles and acorns for the heft of his briefcase and began to swing the big case in circles, just missing my head. Suddenly, the stakes were a lot higher and it occurred to me that what had started as annoyance had now evolved into a situation in which I could genuinely be hurt. I neared the top of the hill but Jeff wasn't done yet and I felt the whoosh of wind near my ear as the briefcase sped past my head.

The spirit that comes from a long line of strong women broke the surface.

That was ... **it**.

As Jeff readied to strike once more I turned and, grasping the handle of my little metal lunchbox with all of my might, swung a right hook that would have made a boxer proud. The corner of the metal box crashed across Jeff's face with my entire will and bodyweight behind it.

As his head snapped back and then came back to center, the look on Jeff's face was one of surprise.

Then the blood started.

It trickled from his nose and then from a gash on his mouth. I stood in silence, lunch box in hand, ready to go should he be stupid enough to engage me again. When it became apparent that he was done for the day, I turned without a word and made for home. I knew that I was in for it, but I also knew that Jeff Russo deserved that bloody nose and felt sure that there had been no alternative. As I neared the house in the late afternoon drizzle, I decided that I would not apologize to him or to anybody for my decision.

I opened the screen door. My mother was on the phone. The person on the other end was obviously Jeff's mother.

"I'm simply amazed that Jenifer would do something so horrible," she was saying as I entered the kitchen. She shot me the look of death.

"This is so out of character for her," she continued, "And we will be speaking with her immediately."

My father sat quietly at the kitchen table. As my mother continued to lament my behavior he looked at me with a grin and whispered, "So you finally gave it to ol' Jeff Russo."

I smiled back.

Within minutes I was grounded, but Jeff Russo never bothered me again.

Years later I asked my father what he thought about fighting.

"Is war okay?" I asked one afternoon. It was the year that I applied to West Point. We were drinking iced tea, sitting outside in the Adirondack chairs that my father built.

"I think we shouldn't go looking for trouble," he said thoughtfully, "but I think when we are threatened we have a right to defend ourselves."

As I surveyed the sawdust pit, I wondered where this scenario figured into the scheme of justified self-defense.

"Put your feet in the straps and pull it up," said the Special Forces instructor.

He was telling me how to don the groin protector and I pulled it up until it sat around my waist with the cup in the front. The straps were tight and they made my thighs stick out like drumsticks. The chest protector was too large for me and shifted left and right as I moved. The helmet bit into my forehead and the elbow and knee pads made it nearly impossible for me to move with any precision.

I looked ridiculous.

I was so self conscious that I wished I could take an etool[27] and dig myself a hole to hide in. But instead I sighed, took a deep breath and faced the center of the ring.

My first opponent was one of the girls I bunked with. We were roughly the same size, but I knew that I had the advantage. I was a girl's girl at heart, with *Vogue* tucked under my mattress, but inside I was a fighter and I suspected that my bunkmate was not.

My roommate and I entered the ring. There were a few jeers about "mud wrestling" from the rest of the platoon. The instructor gave the signal and the duel began. My opponent struck me hard in the chest and won a point, but it was just enough to make me annoyed. With two quick blows to the head, my friend toppled into the sawdust.

---

[27] Entrenching tool carried by soldiers; looks like a folded mini shovel.

I felt elated … and lousy. I helped her to her feet, feeling the urge to apologize as she caught her breath. The instructor saw the look on my face.

"You have to remember Cadet, it's you or them,"

Right. Me or them.

With each round, my classmates advanced or were eliminated. Before long, it was my turn again. This time, however, my opponent was my classmate, Chris Rudimaker. He was small, but wiry and strong. With the massive chest protector sliding around on my torso, the groin cup in place and pugel stick in hand, I entered the circle and instantly knew that I was out of my league.

"C'mon Beaudean, you can do it!" Surprisingly, it was Mike Miller's voice.

As the instructor gave the command, the round began and Chris moved toward me with confidence. I thought I might get in a quick shot to the groin and tried for it with gusto. But Chris's superior strength and my own self-doubt turned the tide. He brought his stick to bear with a mighty left hook to my head.

I dropped to the ground like a sack of potatoes. If I had been a cartoon, the stars would have been circling my head. I lay on my back in the sawdust and fought to bring my mind back in line. Chris won the match.

While my head ached, at least I was now eliminated from the competition. I would not have to fight again. A silver lining. I peeled off all of the hideous gear. But as I unbuckled the chest guard, I couldn't help but think of the more sobering outcome in time of war. If Chris Rudimaker had been the enemy … I would be dead.

13

Beaudean, I can see it in your eyes. You're somewhere else, thinkin' about some other fuckin' thing and you'd better get yourself focused and your head in the game. I want to win today."

Mike Miller's whispered voice broke through my daydreaming. We were standing in accountability formation at the crack of dawn.

"I swear, if I have to put up with your attitude for the next twelve hours, the slide for life is going to be the least of your worries. I'll kill you myself," I whispered.

I could see him grinning out of the corner of my eye. I had reluctantly come to like the son of a bitch.

The competition was Soldiers Fitness Day, the *piece de resistance* of the yearling summer. For the next twelve hours, the platoons would compete in an array of impossible tasks. Mike Miller couldn't wait to get started.

I couldn't wait for it to be over.

At the word "Go!" we raced to the howitzer. The platoon was tasked with pulling the heavy gun nearly half a mile up a hill. My classmates grabbed the ropes on the front. Others were posted on the side, pushing the wheels. I was with a group at the rear, pushing the gun up the steep slope. I placed my butt and back up against the back of the gun and heaved with all of my might. The group strained against the weight. Thirty minutes later we crested the top -- in record time. We were off to a roaring start.

"Fuckin' whooah!" yelled Mike, hardly breathing hard, throwing a fist into the air.

I rolled my eyes.

At the parade field, we ran to the litters lying on the ground. Now we would take turns racing across the field carrying a "wounded" classmate. Teams of three took off with cheers from the rest of the platoon. One classmate rode on the litter as the wounded soldier, while the other two hefted the load and carried the litter to the other end of the field, running all the way.

When it came my turn, I picked up my end. The "victim" was a 220 pound, 6'2" football player. Off we went, across the field. As we reached the halfway point, my heavy classmate looked up at me from the litter.

"C'mon Jen, push it!"

"Say another word and I'll drop you on your head," I panted.

We raced toward the finish line. My arms gave out just as we crossed it and I let go of my end unceremoniously, dropping our "wounded" classmate on the ground below.

"Hey!" he cried.

He forgot his indignation as we applauded our strong performance. The feeling of accomplishment was incredible but short lived.

It was time for the Slide for Life.

I stood at the top of the thirty foot tower. The zipline was stretched from the top of the tower to a point far across the water. Each cadet would step off the tower holding onto a bar and ride the line to the other side. I looked down. The water didn't start for about twenty feet, and there was nothing but rocks and dirt far below.

I'm going to die, I thought.

I looked up.

"I'm going to die," I said to the NCO who was supervising the tower. He looked at me and grinned.

"You're not going to die. Just don't let go."

Don't let go?! This is your big piece of advice?

I looked back at Mike, who was standing on the ladder waiting for his turn.

"No really, I'm going to die right here at the base of the tower."

"Beaudean, are you whining?" asked Mike. His face was filled with challenge, mixed with, what was it, a bit of affection?

"No, I'm serious," I continued, once again looking over the edge, "what if I can't hold on?"

There was fear in my voice.

Mike must have sensed it and he looked back at me -- a long look, reassuring me.

You can do this.

There it was -- my father's voice, that same encouragement, there in my mind.

You can do this.

I looked one last time over the side. All I could see were the rocks below. The team was behind me, cheering me on and waiting for me to go. As usual, the task wasn't optional.

I had tears in my eyes as I stepped off, gripped the bar for dear life and began the ride across the lake. The line zipped loudly as I rode it across, leaving Mike and my platoon mates far behind, picking up speed as I went.

"Ohhhhh Goooooddddddddddddddddd."

My loud cry followed me across the water, down the zipline as I whizzed across the lake. The NCO on the opposite shore had two flags in his hands. As I sped mightily toward the other side, I watched him until he raised the flags. Pulling my legs up so that my body was an L shape, I let go of the bar and dropped butt first into the water.

"Thank you God! Thank you God!"

As I surfaced the words left my lips with no regard for who might hear them.

My body ached but the sense of accomplishment overshadowed it.

Next? The ruck run – a five mile race with all of our gear.

At the pop of the gun, my platoon took off down the road and over the bridge, collectively determined to beat the best time of the day. For the ruck run, the word "run" was the operative word. With our full gear weighting our bodies, our boots pounded the pavement as the group leapt forward, the strongest of the platoon in the front, setting a breakneck pace.

By the first half mile my heart was screaming and I felt it would leap out of my chest. By the end of the first mile, my calves were in knots. By the second mile, the stronger athletes in the group had begun to take my equipment, my canteens and my gas mask. As I struggled to keep up with the dead sprint, the platoon surged forward and Mike called to me between breaths.

"Give me your pack. C'mon, we have to do this together. Let it off your back."

I didn't have to be told twice. I hated that I needed help but I was glad to have it. As we raced along I put my arms straight back behind me and Mike pulled the pack off my back and stacked it on top of his own, carrying two of them along with all of his other gear. With his long legs and lean frame, he easily paced with the rest. My ranger buddy could have run with the fastest of the platoon in the front, but he stayed next to me in the back, never leaving my side, pushing me to keep up.

I had never known such pain. By the third mile my head was tipped back as I sucked in air. I wondered if it was physically possible for my heart to beat any faster. The blood was pounding in my veins and I could feel it in the heat of my cheeks. Tears stung my eyes as I labored to keep up with the platoon. Someone took my rifle from my shoulder, but by this time I was barely aware of my surroundings.

I was far from alone in dragging at the rear. The fastest, strongest in the platoon were setting the pace, while the weaker athletes brought up the rear. But the stronger helped the weaker, shouting encouraging words, helping to carry their equipment.

There were times along the way when my eyes closed for minutes at a time, my legs feeling like rubber beneath me, times where I was barely conscious, barely aware of the bodies next to me. Mike often had my arm, literally pulling me along. To my credit, I kept my spot at the back of the group.

As the start of the fifth mile passed underneath us, there was a tiny ray of light at the end of the tunnel.

"We're almost done," panted Mike, dragging me along, "Just a little bit farther. C'mon, don't give up on me now. You can do it."

The platoon rounded the last half mile and sprinted past the obstacle course toward the parade field. Minutes later we crossed the finish line and I collapsed on the other side. Mike grabbed me by the back of my LBE and pulled me up.

"C'mon, you don't want to cramp up, let's go, walk it off."

It was all I could do to stand.

"You did it Beaudean, un-fucking-believable. I didn't know if you'd hold it together, but you really hung in there. Great job," he said, shaking his head.

"Everybody had to take my gear," I said, nearly weeping, my breath coming in short bursts.

"Everybody had to take everybody's gear," he replied, "There's no shame in that. You did your part and we did ours. Oh for fuck's sake, don't cry now," he said as my eyes welled up.

I pulled it together as we walked along the edge of the field. My breath was returning and with it, my sanity.

With the ruck run finished, the rest of the day seemed more manageable. The platoon gathered at the edge of the lake to build poncho rafts, which would keep our gear dry as we swam across the water. I deftly tied the cords together to form a waterproof bundle. I was a strong swimmer and stringing my boots around my neck, I walked into the water. I knew this was one task I would have well in hand and although it was a long swim across the lake while pushing the raft in front of me, I looked forward to the cool water on my face.

With the water up to my knees, I followed Mike further into the lake.

"Hold on a minute," I said to him and reached to fix the boot laces biting into his neck. I pulled them down under his collar and patted him twice on the back.

"Admit it, you love me," he grinned, looking back over his shoulder.

"Yeah, like a hole in head," I replied, smiling back.

Finally, we were buddies.

Camp Buckner ended a few days later and the yearling class began the long road march back to West Point proper.

"I have to tell ya Beaudean, you surprised me in the end," Mike said over his shoulder.

"Really. How's that?" I replied.

"I really kind of thought you were a loser, y'know, not really meant to be here ... definitely not whooah ... but I have to say, you got better over the summer. Still not great, but better."

I stopped in my tracks and cocked my head to one side.

It was a back-handed compliment, but a compliment nonetheless.

What did one say to a statement like that? Thank you?

But no gratitude was necessary. Mike was already moving forward, negotiating past a fallen log, and I realized that he was really just thinking out loud. He was already talking with the guys about what they really wanted once they were back in garrison. A hot shower and a cold beer, the latter of which they weren't allowed.[28]

"What do you want Beaudean?" Mike called to me, including me in the "what do you look forward to most?" conversation.

Like them, a hot shower. Being clean for more than a few minutes at a time.

---

[28] In order to drink alcohol at West Point, cadets must be both a firstie and 21 years old. Even then, there is no drinking allowed in the barracks.

But really?

Freedom, I thought while I answered something different, something that didn't require explanation.

Freedom from trying to gain everyone's approval.

That's what I really wanted.

Weeks later my mother looked at me over a cup of tea.

"How is it that you of all people, such a free spirit, would pick something so utterly confining?"

I shook my head and said nothing. I was embroiled in the battle now, caught up in my own determination to succeed. How could I explain to my mother that I could never give up, that I had to prove to myself, to my father, to Mike Miller, to Cadet Bailey that I could do this – that I could be a good cadet, a good soldier.

"I'm like a dog with a bone," I replied with a wry smile.

"Hmm," my mother replied, and took a sip.

153 pounds.

I grabbed my rucksack and looked for a moment at Mike Miller's back as he walked away. I hadn't seen the granite of the Academy in nearly three months. I stowed my field gear in my locker in the sinks, found my room assignment and started to pull my trunks up from the basement. The voices of cadets rang out in the barracks, echoing in the empty spaces. The plebes didn't arrive from Lake Frederick until the following day and there was an air of preparation, the start of a new academic year. As the sun set over the Cadet Chapel, I took a break from unpacking and walked across Central Area, through the sallyport, onto the Apron, deep in my own thoughts.

The Plain was green and lush despite the heat. The statue of George Washington on his horse looked out across the stretch toward the bleachers where the "G.A.P.," or the "great American public" would watch the parades on Saturday mornings during football season. I could hear the yearlings from the open windows.

I can't believe I'm here.

But duty called. There was a room to set up and a room-mate to catch up with, a class schedule to get and the training board to look at for the next day, so I turned back into the Area and back into my life as a cadet.

Two years later Mike died in a dunebuggy accident while on Spring Break.

When I heard the news, I wept.

14

First semester, yearling year.

BAM! BAM!

Two knocks, 0515 hours. Jill and I sat up in bed and groaned in unison.

Health and Welfare Inspection.

Barracks rules were very strict. No appliances, no pets, no posters on the walls, and absolutely no drugs or alcohol. The Health and Welfare Inspection was unannounced, twice yearly and always at the crack of dawn. Cadets stood in their pajamas looking on while the command staff and Tactical Officer rifled through drawers and wardrobes looking for contraband and doling out justice for any infraction.

Jill and I owned a space heater, coffee maker, popcorn popper and a toaster. In addition, there was a fifth of vodka in a secret compartment in the overhead bin. We were breaking nearly every rule. We were a first class board[29] waiting to happen.

Jill grabbed the coffee maker to stuff into her lingerie drawer while I stashed the space heater under our makeup bags and the tampons.

"You ready?" Jill whispered, glancing at me.

"Tally ho," I replied wryly.

"ENTER SIR!" we both cried in unison and stood at attention in our sock feet. The door opened and through it marched Major Devlin, the new Tactical Officer, Cadet Bai-

---

[29] Serious infractions such as drinking in the barracks result in a "first class board." Punishment generally includes a slew of demerits and six months of Area tours, which involve walking back and forth across the Area with a rifle for hours on end.

ley, the newly crowned company commander, and the first
sergeant.

Jill and I looked on while the three men began to search
the room. Cadet Bailey opened Jill's desk drawers. The first
sergeant opened my foot locker. The TAC turned to the
overhead closet. But the three men came up empty and left.

"Holy shit, I don't think I took a breath for a full five
minutes," I said.

"This is the day to play the lottery," Jill replied.

Ten minutes later we gathered in the latrine to pee into a little
cup for the urinalysis. The "piss test" was closely monitored
and each cadet was observed urinating into their cup so that
there could be no later claims of tampering. It primarily pro-
tected the cadet being tested since the penalty for a "hot"
urinalysis was instant dismissal for drug use. With my pee in a
jar and carefully labeled, I moved on to the part of the morning I dreaded most.

There were several cadets lined up in front of the scale. I took
my place at the end of the line and tried to look dignified.
Most of all, I tried to look thin.

I stepped on the scale and the first sergeant began to
move the little slider along the numbers. Further and further
it went. I watched in dismay as it finally came to rest on the
heaviest weight of my life. There was a snigger from one of
the cadets in line before me and the color rushed to my face.
The first sergeant looked at the scale again and then wrote the
number down and frowned at me.

156 pounds.

Not good.

It was twenty minutes before lunch formation and the TAC
had called a special meeting. As we gathered on the Area the
music started.

AC/DC's *Back in Black* blasted from the window on the
first floor. We looked up as Cadet Bailey and one of his

classmates slammed open the door from the barracks to the stoops and strode to stand above us on the steps. They both had been victorious, completing Ranger School in a flawless nine weeks and the new Tactical Officer was eager to hold them up as a shining example. Cadet Bailey was now officially invincible and stood at the top of the steps looking like a young god.

Major Devlin had obviously planned the dramatic recognition of the company's new Ranger and his even more obvious purpose was to remind the cadets of Echo Company that each cadet should be striving for lofty goals. Major Devlin was a Ranger himself, a West Point grad, and was as strack as they come. He stood five foot ten inches tall, with his brown hair cut high and tight around his head. His body was lean, and by the way he constantly ran his thumbs along his belt between his shirt and his pants, it was apparent that he reveled in his own fitness. As he publicly congratulated Cadet Bailey on his amazing accomplishment it was clear that he meant to set an equally high standard for the rest of the company.

I looked up to where Cadet Bailey stood on the stoops. He was *perfect* and I knew for certain that he was completely out of my league.

Major Devlin stood there running his thumbs along his waistline.

No doubt he would be trouble.

Matt Bailey. That was his first name. I was a yearling now and no longer the low man on the totem pole. I called upperclass cadets by their first name and the new class of plebes called me "Ma'am." People who had previously referred to me as "Beanhead"[30] were now "Rob" and "Mike." It was exhilarating. Each time I left my room, walking at my leisure down the center of the hallway, chatting with whomever I wished, I felt a little rush. I was still enjoying the fact that plebe year was

---

[30] Slang for plebe.

over. I was also enjoying the change from eight weeks at Camp Buckner -- being clean for more than five minutes at a time.

Everything was going well. Except my weight.

And that was about to change everything.

I recognized his footfall behind me as he made his way to formation.

"You're back," Cadet Bailey said to me.

He sounded ... happily surprised?

Matt looked the same and his shirt proudly displayed the new Ranger tab. He wore the role of company commander like it was made for him.

"The letters you wrote me while I was at Ranger School never said anything about Buckner and I wondered if you had decided to leave," he continued. There was a nice smile on his face, like he was genuinely glad to see me.

"No, I'm back," I said only, smiling back at him.

Then I tried it out.

"I'm back *Matt.*" There it was, his name, rolling out of my mouth.

"Good, this is where you *should* be Jenifer," he commented, like he knew a truth that no one else did and, smiling at me, turned to take his place in formation.

I watched him walk away and wondered what he thought about and *who* he thought about.

The first sergeant called the company to attention and then opened ranks to have shoes, brass, uniforms and haircuts inspected. I had carefully shined my hat brass and shoes and they looked good. When the platoon leader turned to look at my uniform he took a cursory look at my shoes and launched into ...

"Heard you didn't make weight this morning," he said.

His voice had been quiet, but not that quiet. I knew that my classmates around me could hear the conversation.

Yes, I know you know. I know you know I'm fat. Now you know I know you know. Now everybody knows!

That evening, with four fellow "disappointees" who had also failed the weigh-in, I reported for the next step in the fat cadet nightmare -- the "taping."

The female platoon leader who had watched me pee that morning wrapped a measuring tape around my waist and hips. She measured my neck and then my wrist, then my forearm. Each measurement was repeated three times. I felt the tape touch the round part of my butt and wiggled uncomfortably.[31]

She carefully wrote each number on a clipboard. I felt my stomach sink. I could read upside down. I wasn't going to make it.

It was official. I was now on the dreaded Weight Program.

Later that night there was a knock on the door.

It was Matt Bailey.

"This is a nice surprise," I said amiably.

"Hi. Got a minute?" he asked. He looked uncomfortable.

I looked at him and the way his jeans sat on his hips. Sometimes the "something" between us was palpable. But even if he had ever returned my feelings of admiration and affection, I doubted that he would allow himself to act on them. I sensed that Matt Bailey needed a girlfriend who was physically perfect, not too assertive or independent minded, definitely not a cadet.

"I saw your name on the list for the Weight Program," he started.

He paused as if struggling with his choice of words and then continued.

---

[31] The assumption was that even if a cadet was over the limit in weight, if they were in terrific physical shape and doing a great deal of weight lifting, their body fat percentage would be low and they would meet the requirement through this additional screening method.

"It's going to make your life a lot more difficult if you don't get it under control."

I worked to keep my face professional to hide my hurt. I looked at the curve of his jaw and the strength of his stance as he leaned against the rifle rack. He had a tiny hint of a gut around his waist. He was putting weight back on after nine weeks of near starvation at Ranger School, but with a few beers too many at the Firstie Club it wasn't landing in all the right places.

But that didn't matter. He hadn't failed the weigh in.

"Unfortunately this is the first thing that the new TAC now knows about you," he continued, "and your classmates won't respect it if you can't get a handle on it. As your company commander, I don't like to see any member of the company on the weight program. I think if you just eat less …."

He tapered off.

Eat less. See, I never thought of that.

I nodded slowly.

I wanted to give him hell for his lack of support and encouragement. But wisdom took over. I knew that I needed to be cautious. After all, this wasn't the dialogue of a supportive friend. This wasn't friendship at all. The message was clear -- the message of a Company Commander. Make weight and do it quick.

I looked at him and said with enthusiasm, "I know I need to beat this. I'm committed to losing the weight. I'll make it happen."

Matt listened to my profession of commitment, seemed satisfied and turned to go.

The sun was barely breaking the horizon a few mornings later as I rose for the first official weigh-in of the West Point Weight Program. Jill was asleep and I put my Gym Alpha sneakers on quietly and slipped out the door. The Corps was silent except for the fourth class who were already running around their company areas delivering newspapers and readying for another day of knowledge and table duties. I walked quickly through the tunnel under the Mess Hall and made my way up to the Gym to stand in line with the rest of the weight flunkies.

When it came my turn I stepped up in my sock feet to be weighed and watched as the little slider on the scale slid far to my right.

156 pounds.

The captain waved me over to the taping station and I dutifully reported to the Major who was doing the taping.

"Good morning Cadet Beaudean," he said.

"Good morning Sir."

Not really one good fucking thing about it.

"Let's do your hips first," he continued, "Stand up straight and put your arms away from your sides."

I did as I was told.

In a businesslike fashion he wrapped the tape around my ass right at the level of my hipbone and wrote the measurement down. Then he performed the measurement twice more just to be sure. He measured my neck and my wrist and my forearm and scribbled the numbers onto the paper. He used a calculator to figure my body fat percentage and wrote down the final number.

"See you in four weeks," he said.

"Yes Sir," I replied, "Good morning Sir."

"Next!" he called.

As a member of the West Point's Weight Program, my name was on a list outside the Orderly Room for all to see. Not making weight carried with it a tremendous stigma. It was official. I was a loser. And fixing the problem was an individual sport.

But there was no greater motivation than public humiliation to make me get serious. I began the official attack on my weight. I was determined to find a successful outcome, determined to improve the way I was perceived and, most of all, consumed by the promise that I would never, *ever* go through this again.

I met with the nutritionist and our company trainer. The nutritionist discussed portion size and I signed up for the company "diet table," where dessert was non-fat Jell-O and salad was a staple. The trainer helped me learn more about how to optimally burn calories, tacking a long walk onto the end of a threemile run to keep my heart rate up and adding another cardio workout each day with a swim in the morning before breakfast. I switched to a small bowl of cereal for breakfast, and snacked only on air popped popcorn.

And slowly the pounds came off.

But the reality was that with my medium frame and genetic makeup, I would never be skinny. The most I could hope for was a fit, athletic body. And my health was unfortunately the least of my focus. Staying off the hideous weight program and out of the eye of the chain of command was the only goal.

It was worth any price.

Whatever the cost, I had to make weight.

It was a bitter cold morning in January when I walked through the tunnel under the Mess Hall and up to the gym for the post-Christmas weigh in. I could see my breath against the night sky but I didn't notice the cold. My sole objective was to get off the Weight Program. I had thought of little else for months.

I stepped onto the scale and weighed a nice, neat 142 pounds.

The weight limit for my age and height was 134, so I still wasn't thin enough by weight. But my workouts paid off. My body fat percentage was well beneath the standard. It was worth every Christmas cookie I had forgone.

"Good job Cadet Beaudean," the Captain said with a nod, like I was finally up to par, "Keep it up and don't go out and eat ice cream now."

Y'know what ... fuck you.

"Yes Sir, thank you Sir," I replied.

As I walked toward the door I paused to look back at some of my classmates. A few looked crestfallen. They hadn't made weight and would continue on the program.

"God bless 'em," I thought and turned to go in a flood of relief.

It was still night and the cadet area was deserted as I made my way along McArthur Barracks and back through the tunnel under the Mess Hall.

I did a little victory dance as I walked to the barracks.

My one thought?

I would never go through this again ... *not ever* ... I would die first.

15

W hat's wrong?" Jill asked.
I could hear the worry in her voice.
"I don't know. Get Matt," I choked.

I lay in bed shaking like a leaf. I was freezing and my teeth chattered. I couldn't breathe. As Matt sat down on the edge of the bed I could smell his scent -- very clean, a little sweet. He took my hand.

"I can't ... catch my breath," I choked.

"Loosen her clothes," he said to Jill.

He unzipped my dress grey jacket. I could hear the sirens of the approaching ambulance. Twenty minutes later we were in the Emergency Room. I looked up from the gurney as the nurses rolled me away to see Matt where I had left him – standing there, looking after me.

It had been cold in the Hudson Valley that afternoon, threatening snow. Despite the temperature and a Calculus exam the next day, I went out to the USMA stables to ride. I was dressed in a pair of old jeans, heavy boots, a thick red sweater and a barn jacket. The good humored gelding trotted along and we made our way up to a lookout on one of the mountains. We reached the top and I patted the horse on the neck as I leaned on the front of the saddle to look across the water. The view was spectacular. I could see the Bear Mountain Bridge and the river. The freeze was underway and small ice floes were beginning to form. At the top of the mountain the Weight Program and academics were distant. I had five seconds to myself. Here was a small taste of freedom.

"Jenny, how are you?" he asked.

I was dismounting outside the barn and turned to look at a classmate from my Calculus class.

"Hello Dave," I replied with a smile as my feet hit the ground with a thud.

"Are you all set for the exam tomorrow?" he asked.

"I've studied some," I replied.

"Some" meant less prepared than I should have been. My plan was to cram the bulk of the studying into the coming evening.

"We have a study group meeting tonight if you want to join us," he continued.

"How is the preparation going?" I asked, pulling the bridle off the horses' head.

"It sucks, and I have to say, the last section has a lot more material than I thought. I have a long way to go tonight."

I looked at him, tiny seeds of worry beginning to sprout in my mind.

"I thought his last two lectures made up the smaller section of the exam," I replied with hope in my voice.

"No, remember the last class? He said that he was going to put the most points in the material from the last section," Dave replied slowly.

He watched the self-doubt pass across my face. His look held understanding -- and just a tiny bit of pity. I pulled the saddle off the gelding in a quick motion, determined to get back to the barracks as quickly as possible so that I could re-assess the situation.

Maybe the time I had would be enough.

With a sense of impending doom I took the stairs two at a time and burst through the door to my room. Jill looked up in surprise. I grabbed my Calculus assignment book and turned to the page that explained the exam. Sure enough, it covered substantial content for which I hadn't planned. I looked at the clock, calculating how long I would need to prevent a failing grade.

"How did I miss this?" I chided myself.

Stay calm.

"How could I be so stupid?"

Minutes before I had been riding, happy as a lark.

Now I was in math hell.

Jill and I walked out to the Sunday night accountability formation, pausing in front of the full length mirror near the door to check the spotlessness of our shirts and coats. I examined the way my trousers sat on my thighs and wished the line of my leg was smoother. Thinner.

141 pounds.

"Try not to stress," suggested Jill as we walked down the steps, "Remember Kat's 'Expandable Homework Theory.' The work you need to get done takes exactly as much time as you have."

I tried to latch on to her positive attitude but my anxiety was turning into something palpable, something I didn't recognize. I already had a low average in the class. I began to imagine the worst. To fail the exam meant potentially failing the class. To fail the class meant STAP.[32] If a cadet failed a class twice, God forbid, the cadet was separated -- no questions asked.

The first sergeant called the company to attention but I hardly heard his words for the ringing in my ears. My lips were tingling and my nose was ice cold. My heart began to beat faster and then pound, as if it would come out of my chest. There were dots in front of my eyes. I couldn't catch my breath.

Before the first sergeant could say another word, I sank to the pavement.

The ER physician looked down at me where I lay with a mildly sympathetic gaze.

"What you had is an anxiety attack," he explained, "It's the fight or flight response manifesting itself. The good news is that there's nothing wrong with you."

---

[32] Summer school.

"I couldn't breathe. I felt like I was going to die," I responded.

How could there be nothing wrong with me?

"The attacks feel real enough when they happen, but they are not physiologically threatening in any way. You're probably just responding to stress. Is there something going on in your life that is causing you stress?"

I looked at him incredulously. Was this a joke?

"Cadet *life* is a little stressful," I replied with a hint of sarcasm.

"Well, obviously today was more stressful than usual," he replied, "We'll keep you for observation tonight and then what you probably need is some rest tomorrow."

I nodded but was already wondering what I was going to tell Matt Bailey. I had just passed out in formation and had a ride to the hospital in an ambulance. How the hell did I explain to Matt that this was nothing?

But before I could think more about it, the evening took a turn I had never imagined possible.

"Do you feel better now?" the doctor asked.

His voice had changed. It was soft, sensual. He was running the back of his hand up and down my arm, brushing the side of my breast.

Suddenly I could feel his erection against my hip.

My brow crinkled in confusion and in disbelief. I moved his hand away, hoping that I had misinterpreted his touch.

But I hadn't -- and the night was just beginning.

0100 hours. He appeared again.

"How are you feeling now?" he asked. His voice was like a caress. He leaned against me, rubbing his crotch against my leg, touching my breasts, his soft voice suggestive and unmistakable. He tried to put my hand on his penis but I yanked it away.

0230 hours. He was back. And again at 0330. Every time I nodded off to sleep the good doctor appeared at my bedside. I would wake with a start to find his hands on me, his words making excuses to touch me. Twice I thought he would kiss me.

Morning arrived and I was released. Matt was sitting on the couch in the waiting room and rose to his feet as I walked out to meet him.

"Are you okay?" he asked.

I nodded.

"Good," he nodded wearily. He looked tired.

In the Army truck back to the barracks, we said nothing. Matt had spoken to the doctor, who explained that dehydration and exhaustion were to blame for my visit to the hospital. The doctor probably seemed like a good guy and I'm sure it never occurred to Matt that anything inappropriate had occurred. As for me, I was completely exhausted – more from fending off the doctor's sexual advances than from the anxiety attack.

"Thanks for taking me to the hospital," I said as the truck pulled up outside Central Guard Room.

"No sweat," he answered, "Get some rest, okay."

It was now past breakfast and I was hungry. I hadn't eaten since lunch the previous day and stopped at the Cadet Mess to pick up a bran muffin left over from breakfast. I walked slowly back to the barracks and as I opened the door to sign in at the Orderly Room, Matt was standing in the hallway at the opposite end of the corridor, making some notes on a pad. He looked up. He made no allusion to the adventure of the night before. Instead, he looked at the muffin in my hand and then back at the pad of paper he was holding.

"Do you really think you should be eating a muffin? How about fruit?" he asked.

He was alluding to my weight, the never-ending focus on my *fucking* weight.

"You have <u>got</u> to be kidding me," I yelled at him.

I had just had a panic attack, passed out in formation, been taken to the hospital, been sexually assaulted by the E.R. doctor and still had to figure out what to do about the Calculus exam – all in twelve hours. I was in no mood for any kind of bullshit. I visualized the muffin hurling through space to meet his forehead but to act on such an impulse would be unthinkable. Instead, I gave him a disgusted look, pitched the offending muffin into the nearby trashcan and left him standing there with a bewildered look on his face.

In the safety of my room I stripped off my clothes and threw them on the floor in a pile. I crawled into my bed and closed my eyes. I was too tired even to cry.

Later that afternoon Jill sat on the end of my bed and listened with disbelief as I relayed the tale of unsolicited romance at Kelleher Army Hospital.

"Unbelievable," said Jill, "I mean really unbelievable, like un-fucking-believable. What a freak."

"I know, that's how I felt, like I was imagining it as Dr. Hard-On felt me up," I mused. "I knew I should say something but there was no one to say anything to! The whole time I kept thinking, 'Where the hell is everyone?' But even if the nurses were there, this guy is an officer and there's a good chance that no one would believe me. I was just so humiliated. It was awful."

"You should have thrown that muffin at Matt," she continued.

"He was very caring really. Matt, I mean … affectionate even."

"There's something there, no question Jenny. I've seen the way he looks at you."

We sat on the bed together, thinking.

"What are you going to do about the asshole doctor?" asked Jill.

"I'm not sure what to do about it," I replied wearily. "If I report it, then it causes a big mess for Doctor Hard-On, but it really causes a bigger mess for me. There would be an investigation, blah, blah, blah. I just don't need that kind of attention right now."

A sexual harassment charge against an Army officer would spread through the cadet rumor mill like a fire on dry grass.

Jill nodded. She understood.

I looked up at my friend and mused, "Maybe I can just scare the crap out of him," and described my plan.

After a good night's sleep, miraculous completion of the Calculus exam and a three mile run, I was feeling like a new woman and empowered. I sat on the stoops with my feet up on a chair admiring the day and crafted the following note:

Dear Dr. Rancin,

You treated me last weekend in the ER at Kelleher. During my overnight stay, you took it upon yourself to take advantage a difficult situation by touching me inappropriately in what should be a strictly professional relationship between doctor and patient. As a cadet, I frankly don't have the time to deal with the situation properly and report it as the incident certainly deserves. So instead, I send you the following warning. Female cadets have a habit of exchanging stories in all their vivid detail around the locker room and through their network of friendships. That said, if I ever hear any rumor that you have taken similar liberties with another female cadet, I will report you and your actions immediately to the chain of command and ensure that you are properly prosecuted.

I looked up to see Jill walking up to me.

I handed her the note.

"Well, that ought to do it," she said after she had read it, "Hopefully that will make him think twice before doing it again."

That afternoon I took the bus to Kelleher Army Hospital and watched West Point roll by as the bus cruised past Eisenhower Hall, the Catholic Chapel and the Cemetery. The note sat on my lap in a crisp, white envelope. When it was safely delivered to the InBox of the good doctor, I felt a sense of satisfaction that I had put the situation to bed in the way that made the most sense. It allowed me to continue with my life without a scandal and while hopefully curbing Dr. Hard-On's sexual liberties. The doctor would always know that somewhere out there was a young female cadet who could ruin his career and his life. It seemed punishment enough.

I stepped off the bus in front of the library and walked to the roof of Thayer Hall. The building is enormous and stands like a fortress facing the Hudson River. The roof is a parking lot for the officers who teach in the building. It is also a great spot to take in a fabulous view of the river.

I walked to the edge and leaned on the granite railing. The river lay long and dark with films of ice running along its sides. It was beautiful. West Point is a stunner, no question, even in the dead of winter, when everything – the sky, the buildings, the water – match the grey of the cadets.

Turning from the view, I did my best to leave the incident in the E.R. behind. I needed to focus on the more pressing requirements of my life as a cadet. As for the anxiety attack, it didn't raise its ugly head again – at least for a while.

The months passed and Graduation Day dawned clear, sunny and spectacular. I sat in the stands in Michie Stadium with the rest of the plebes, yearlings and cows and watched as Matt Bailey and his classmates received their diplomas. When the class was dismissed, the white hats flew up in the air and I watched in wonder. The distance between me and such an accomplishment seemed impossible.

Making my way down to the field, I found Matt Bailey. We looked at each other for a long moment. Then he hugged and held me. There was little time to say much, and even if there had been, I didn't have the words. I wasn't a girlfriend. I wasn't sure I was even a friend. Who knew what defined this odd relationship of two years. Hero worship? Or mutual affection between leader and subordinate? Either way, the time was past and as it is common for cadets to salute the newly graduated second lieutenants, I lifted my hand to the brim of my hat.

He returned the salute and said quietly, "I'll miss ya kid."

"I'll miss you too," I replied. I wanted to touch his face, to tell him everything.

Instead, I watched him walk away.

He paused to talk to a classmate but he turned and saw me looking and gave me a smile and a wave. I waved back.

Good luck Matt. I love you.

Another year finished. I was halfway done.

But yearling year had taken its toll. Camp Buckner, followed by a tough year of academics, the hideous Weight Program and the never-ending grind of cadet life, had drained me. Even with the thrill of watching the firsties graduate, I had had about all the "good military training" I could take. If the doubts and misgivings by themselves were not enough, as Kat and I pinned on each other's third year cow brass, I looked ahead to the next challenge with a sense of discouragement. Summer assignments had been posted and I was assigned to Camp Buckner …again …this time as a squad leader.

For the first time I thought seriously about leaving the Academy.

16

I think this looks terrific and I think it's time for a change," my mother said.

She propped the brochure for Gettysburg College on the kitchen counter and read it while she stirred a batch of cookie dough. I looked over her shoulder and nodded.

"Maybe we can go visit," I replied through a mouthful.

"I think you need to finish your commitment though," my father said, looking over his glasses. He had been deep in the New York Times, but apparently not that deep.

"Camp Buckner is only two weeks away," he continued, "How would they get another one of your classmates in place to lead your squad in that short amount of time? You'd be leaving them in the lurch."

"It's the *Army* Jack, I'm sure they'll *survive*," replied my mother, rolling her eyes.

"Just the same, I think you should finish what you started," my father continued firmly, "Gettysburg will be there at the end of the summer."

"Okay," I replied, looking at my father.

Four days later I was back at Camp Buckner for T cubed.[33]

I leaned down from where I sat on my bunk and laced up my boots. This was my "second" pair, the pair not spit shined for inspection but simply brush shined a dull black for a night tromping through the woods. I grabbed my gear – my LBE with all the requisite equipment -- two canteens full of water, ammo pouches and poncho. I put on my steel pot, which held my map in its headband and swung the gear over my

---

[33] "Train the trainer" is two to three weeks of preparation for the cadre who will lead the yearling class through the training at Camp Buckner.

shoulder. The metal door crashed closed behind me as I walked out to formation for a long night of land navigation and patrolling. We had spent every minute of the last two weeks brushing up on tactical knowledge, learning to teach classes on various military tactics and doing monstrous amounts of PT -- all with the purpose of providing the yearling class with a "whooah" first four weeks of Camp Buckner.

The critical difference with this Camp Buckner versus the last was the state and strength of my body. I had worked hard at the gym over the past year and was now in the best shape of my life. I could pound out five miles at a nice clip and could knock out a respectable 50 pushups in two minutes.

138 pounds.

This single change was about to pay off in a way I could never have imagined.

I walked out to where the rest of the cadre were standing and looked up just in time to catch the platoon tactical officer adjusting himself.

Did that man just fix his balls in front of me?

But the Major didn't seem to care that the only female in the 1st Platoon cadre was privy to the position of his genitals. Major Daniel Tibbins was assigned to oversee T-cubed for 1st Platoon and was coincidentally my French professor from the previous semester. Tibbins was also a chauvinist and a braggart. He felt that women didn't belong in the Army and didn't hesitate to verbalize his conviction. He was a confirmed bachelor and found women a pleasant amusement – particularly Parisian women. In French, Major Tibbins would pontificate about women in the city of lights. French women were stylish and sexy. French women were so feminine. French women had beautiful, round bottoms. Blah, blah, blah.

I was reasonably fluent and I got the gist.

During T-cubed classes on machine gun assembly, patrolling in a wedge formation, donning gas masks and recognizing enemy aircraft, Tibbins seemed eager to forget that I existed.

It didn't take much to push me over the edge.

"This fucking blows," my ranger buddy yelled to me where I stood fifty feet behind him with the compass. We were in the middle of the forest by ourselves with a map and a compass, finding points for land navigation.

"You ain't seen nothing yet," I called back as I looked up. The first raindrop fell and I hurried to get my map into its plastic case.

In minutes we were soaked.

By two in the morning the rain and cloud cover had turned the woods inky black. We joined the rest of the cadre to patrol a route along a riverbed. Our task was to cover several clicks before dawn without being detected by the tactical officers who were posted along the route to play the part of the enemy.

The rain came down with a determined pelt. The water ran down my gear and the middle of my back. It dripped off the front of my helmet and soaked through the laces of my boots, into my socks. I dropped to one knee as the firstie on point called for the group to halt.

Suddenly a flare went up. The "enemy" was trying to find us. The sky glowed bright, the sheets of rain now silver and shiny against the light. We dropped to the ground and lay silent in the wet leaves, careful to avoid detection. As the light from the flare died, we rose and quietly crept on, and the temperature dropped again.

The firstie on point held up a fist. The sign was passed back person to person and I dropped and took a knee as the group halted to consult the map. With my rifle at the ready I leaned against a tree. The bark was rough against my face. It smelled like moss and woodsy fungus. The water ran in little streams down my back.

"You know what they say Cadet Beaudean?"

Tibbins had come up behind me and was whispering.

"What's that Sir?" I asked.

"You know you're truly wet when the water runs down the crack in your ass."

"Yes Sir," I replied dutifully.

"And besides," he continued, "this is good training. All assaults take place uphill at night in the pouring rain where four map sheets come together."

I nodded and tried to hide both my shivering and my aversion for the man.

Gettysburg College was looking better and better.

At 0400 hours, with a successful patrol completed, we walked back into the company area.

"Mademoiselle Beaudean," Major Tibbins addressed me cheerfully in French, "You look like a wet *lapin.*[34] This is good Army training, *Oui?*"

How do you say fuck you in French?

With the obligatory, "Yes Sir, Good morning Sir," I made my way to the barracks to stuff wads of newspaper in my boots to dry them out. I stood in the hot shower with my hands against the wall. The warm water washed away the chill of the night's adventure. I thought about all of the accomplishments of the last two years – and the hours of misery.

I prayed.

Lord, I don't know whether I'm supposed to stay at this place or move on. I need a sign. If you want me at West Point, then you're going to need to let me know.

I figured that the Almighty might forgive the ultimatum given the circumstances.

The next morning the yucks[35] returned from summer leave.

In contrast to the evening's downpour, the day was dawning without a cloud in the sky. I pulled on my shorts and t-shirt and made my way to formation. Even at 0520 hours it was hot. I walked down the line of my newly assigned year-

---

[34] Rabbit.

[35] Slang for yearlings or second year cadets.

lings, looking over their uniforms, and paused in front of the yearling on the end.

"Make sure you do a better job shaving tomorrow morning, okay?"

My message wasn't harsh, just matter of fact. I expected the yearlings in my squad to look sharp. I wasn't interested in being popular and was determined to do a good job leading the squad before I resigned to get on with the rest of my life. My voice was low but the yearling realized immediately that it wasn't a passing comment.

"I will," he replied.

"Good. Thanks," I replied. Smiling at him, I walked away.

I suspected that the yearlings, worn from two weeks of partying while on leave, would suffer through the coming four mile run.

But no matter. I was ready.

The first sergeant called the company to attention, took accountability and turned the ranks with a "right face." Minutes later, the company was running in step with the first sergeant calling the cadence.

By the third mile, the sun was rising with determination. The heat blistered down as the company ran and the smell of alcohol began to reek off the skin of the sweating yearlings. I knew they were hung over, likely dehydrated, and on a brisk four mile run on a hot morning. I grinned. For once I had an advantage.

I could tell the first sergeant was ready for a break.

It was now or never.

Picking up my pace, I left my spot with the platoon and raced up to where he was running beside the company. With a strong voice I took over as he stepped aside. The company picked up my jodie[36] in unified chant.

C-130 rolling down the strip
Airborne ranger gonna take a little trip

---

[36] A Military cadence call.

Mission top secret, destination unknown
Don't even know if we're ever comin' home

For nearly a mile the company ran in step to my call. By the end of my turn I was winded, but my body was strong and I commanded the company with confidence. As we wound back toward the entrance to Camp Buckner, one of the other squad leaders tapped me on the shoulder and I moved aside to allow him to take over.

As I slowed my pace to take a spot at the back of the company I noticed Major Tibbins wheezing with exertion and struggling to keep up. I hid my smile.

Ahhh, there is justice in the world.

When the run was over we released the yearlings to shower and the cadre gathered around the first sergeant to go over the plan for the day. I joined the group and my colleagues welcomed me with clapping hands.

"Jenny, you were large and in charge out there," the platoon leader laughed, "You kicked some serious ass."

The rest of the cadre nodded in agreement.

I beamed.

With one simple athletic performance I had won instant credibility that set the stage for the next four weeks.

For the next twenty seven days the thrill never let up. I set high standards for my squad. The eight yearlings stepped up without hesitation and never questioned my direction. My potential to teach and lead began to blossom and with each day I remembered why I had come to West Point in the first place. I was respected. My opinion was sought. I received top marks from Tibbins and the company leadership. What began as a dreaded assignment ended in a high and a new conviction about my life in the military.

The last day of the detail arrived too soon and I walked back from the snack bar with nine pints of ice cream. My squad sat in easy companionship, some on the bunks, some on the floor, exchanging stories from the last four weeks and laughing together. I looked at each of their faces. I loved each of them -- each with their individual strengths and weaknesses, each with their own quirks. I was proud to be their leader. As the spoons neared the bottoms of the cardboard ice cream cartons, I looked at them all and decided I owed them the truth.

"I hate to leave you all tomorrow," I said slowly. The room quieted.

"You've all said some nice things to me today. That means a great deal to me. I think we've accomplished some good things together during the last four weeks."

They nodded in assent. I paused and took a deep breath.

"Before you all arrived, I had made the decision to resign," I said.

There was an audible gasp and looks of surprise.

"Yearling year was a tough year for me – in a lot of ways. I forgot why I came to West Point in the first place. So I looked at some other colleges and decided that I would finish the detail and then resign. But you've changed that. In the last four weeks I remembered what I love about leadership. Being a squad leader to all of you has been an honor ... and a privilege. I see now that I belong here and I thank you all for reminding me of that."

It never again occurred to me to resign.

Two weeks later, in the best shape of my life, I flew to Army Air Assault School at Camp Gruber, Oklahoma. I had trained hard for the school with the hope that finally I would have a badge to add to my uniform. Rumor had it that the obstacle course at Buckner was similar to the one at Camp Gruber, so I had practiced it repeatedly to get ready. I was determined to be prepared.

On the first day of Air Assault School at Camp Gruber the skies opened up and the rain fell over the course. Whether it was the slick obstacles that made the difference or whether my strength simply wasn't up to the task was hard to determine. Whatever the reason, I failed the obstacle course and therefore the school on the first day. The triumph of Camp

Buckner was instantly gone and I boarded the plane back to West Point in shame.

I stood in front of my tactical officer's desk at the position of attention. He looked up from some papers and gave me a withering look. He wanted an explanation.

"I can't believe you failed out of Air Assault on the first day," he commented over his glasses.

This was the same man who had come out to Buckner and praised my performance. But that all disappeared now with the shame of failure from Air Assault. No matter that the National Guardsmen running the school at Camp Gruber would give failing marks to nearly a third of the cadets in the Air Assault class that summer. Right now the only thing that mattered was that I had failed on the first day, had taken a valuable military school slot that could have gone to someone (apparently) more worthy and would now be expected to hang my head in humiliation and contrition.

"What happened out there?" he asked.

I looked back at him with a steady gaze.

I wasn't about to apologize.

"Sir, I am in arguably the best shape of my life," I replied, "I go to the gym and I run constantly. I'm at my lowest weight since R Day. I worked out hard during my detail at Buckner and practiced the obstacle course to make sure I was ready for Air Assault. I trained and prepared. I gave it my best shot and unfortunately it didn't work out. That's what happened."

He looked at me for a moment. My answer was fifty words too many. What he really expected was "No excuse Sir." He expected me to prostrate myself. Any statement that failure was okay didn't jive with his philosophy that failure was not an option.

He gave me a long look.

"Not acceptable," he replied.

"Yes Sir."

What else could I say?

The room was quiet and then he began again.
"Maybe if you lost a little more weight."
I looked at him in disbelief.

136 pounds.

17

Y ou're goin' down," he grunted.

"Kiss my ass," I panted in reply.

His sweat soaked shirt pressed against my face. I turned to pass the basketball to a teammate and dodged under my opponent's arms. He turned and slammed into my chest, sending me through the air. I hit the floor and slid across the court. From the sidelines there were voices calling for a foul but play didn't stop. I dusted myself off and got back in the game.

The Army believes that sports build the competitive edge that helps the military win on the battlefield. At West Point, intramurals are mandatory. We were required to participate in an intramural each semester and could play the same sport only twice while at the Academy. The Department of Physical Education wanted us to learn new skills and take on new physical challenges.

And if the game had a great deal of physical contact?

Even better!

This philosophy was summarized in a slightly different manner by Kat's description of the intramural program -- "This fucking sucks."

My intramural selection for the semester was three-on-three basketball, which was more than a contact sport -- it was a *combat* sport. With only three players on the court at one time, every cadet played at least half the game. I had no gift for basketball. But I manned the court with knees bent, feet spread, arms outstretched and face beet red from exertion. The bruises on my butt and thighs were testimony to my determination. I might not win in the end, but I'd go down swinging.

As the buzzer went off, Company E-1 lost the game by one shot. But it had been a good fight. The gym began to clear and I looked to the other side. My afternoon wasn't over.

The "shelf" was calling my name.

Every year the Athletic Department at West Point set up the Indoor Obstacle Course Test (IOCT), an athletic examination that all cadets were required to pass. At the word "Go," two cadets at a time raced toward a set of horizontal bars set up off the floor and dropped to low crawl underneath them. Then there was a vault. The third obstacle was a shelf, six or seven feet long and at least four feet wide, suspended by iron bars from the track level that ran around the gym on the second floor. A cadet reached or jumped up, grabbed the edge of the shelf, threw a leg up over the edge and pulled themselves up. From there they went on to complete a slew of other challenges, including a set of monkey bars that were so old they squeaked and turned, a vertical rope climb, a jump and climb over a wall and several laps around the track. Grades were based on time.

It was your basic nightmare.

And of all the obstacles, the shelf was my biggest challenge.

With the cadets heading back for dinner, the lights were dimming and I could hear the last intramural boxing match in progress in the gym below. I was alone. Walking over to the shelf, I half expected a spotlight to shine from above, highlighting the contortions I was about to employ.

Ladies and gentlemen, in the center ring ...

On any given day I only had enough upper body strength for one shot at the shelf. The strength required for just one try would so tire my arms that another attempt would be fruitless. And I had to jump to even reach the edge of the shelf, so my height was a factor as well. Bottom line? I had to get it right the first time.

I positioned myself under the edge of the shelf with my hands raised over my head, my fingertips nearly ten inches from the surface. Jumping up with all of my might, I grabbed the edge and pulled up into a half pull-up, which was as far as my strength would take me. Then I used my abdominal muscles to pull my body into a tight ball with the tips of my toes touching the underside of the shelf. Gripping the lip of the board with all my might, I wiggled my right toe up and over the edge, locking my right heel in the lip. I pulled until the edge of the shelf was at my crotch. Folding my right thigh over the edge of the shelf I pulled with my hands, leg and foot and heaved myself onto the top.

Success.

I rested for a minute and then grabbed the edge of the shelf to swing myself back onto the gym floor. It had been a good day. I had run 3 miles, played basketball and conquered the shelf.

The next morning I weighed myself.

Somehow, I had gained two pounds.

143.

The New York Times hit the floor outside my barracks room door as the paper plebe made his rounds. Someone else was now paying their dues and completing the endless list of chores. I was running late and apparently so was the paper plebe. He would have the pleasure of hearing about the newspaper's late arrival at breakfast formation. But not from me. I had other things on my mind.

I wasn't much of a haze. As long as my plebes were doing their job, learning their knowledge and working hard to prepare their uniforms and their room, I was satisfied. My standard was high but I wasn't about to make their lives miserable. The pressures of life as a cadet were misery enough without help from me. It was my opinion that squad leaders were meant to be teachers and I took that role seriously.

Each morning, my two plebes arrived promptly at ten minutes after six and stood outside the door at parade rest.

I'd prop the door open to ninety degrees with the trashcan, in keeping with the "Matt Bailey system." Kat and I got dressed behind the door and out of sight while I drilled the plebes on their knowledge. Kat had a different assignment that semester and had no plebes she was responsible for, but she helped with mine nonetheless.

"Tell me about the Infantry," I called as I stood behind the door and pulled on my trousers.

"Ma'am, the mission of the Infantry is to close with and destroy the enemy ..."

There was a pregnant pause.

"Using fire and maneuver, right? I thought we were going to get that set for today," I mused, sticking my head around the barricade of the door so that I could make eye contact.

"Yes Ma'am," the plebe replied, knowing full well he was in the wrong.

"That's pretty piss poor," Kat commented.

"I couldn't have said it better myself Cadet McNeil," I replied.

"It takes a village," she grinned.

"Listen you two!" I said with mild irritation, looking up from where I was sitting on the bed tying my low quarters, "It sounds like you're unprepared this morning and need to get your act together. So why don't you *do* that and get the mission of the infantry straight along with the Days and the Corps and everything else that seems to be in a little bit of a mess this week. You have until tomorrow morning, when we meet at 0550 hours -- and this time it had better be right!"

"Yes, Ma'am," the two yelled in unison.

"Ok, get out of here," I called.

The two plebes executed a right face and raced down the edge of the hallway, making a mad dash for the nearest classmate's door. I was already thinking about something else. The IOCT was just one week away.

Kat and I stood in front of the full length mirror just inside the door to the stoops. I tugged at my grey jacket and looked at my body in disgust. After my summer of athletic prowess, my weight was again creeping up. Kat, on the other hand, was the picture of perfection. Her blond knot was neatly pinned under the base of her garrison cap. Her long legs looked lean in her ME Trou, which were loose on her. Her jacket fit nicely. She looked sharp.

If I were gay, I'd be in love with Kat.

It seemed like Kat could go for days without eating. Days. But try as I might to starve myself, I could never endure the torture.

144 pounds.

One week later I stood in the old gym at the starting line for the IOCT.

"GO!" the instructor cried.

I was off.

Low crawl under the bars, up, over the vault.

*Run up to the shelf, jump up, grab the edge, pull up, stomach muscles, make myself into a little ball, hook the foot, pull up, shelf into the crotch, right thigh folded on top, push, push, **push,** torso on top.*

Cross the bars, jump to the floor …

Suspended tire. Jump, grab, pull through.

Balance beam. Walk carefully, be deliberate, better slow than falling.

The wall. Run hard, plant the foot in the center, grab the top, pull up, throw the right leg over, down the other side.

Horizontal ladder, jump up and grab, swing the body right, now left, grab the next bar, swing the body right, now left, grab the next bar ….

Vertical rope climb. Grab the rope, grip the rope with your feet. Stand up. Grab the rope up higher, grip, stand up. Repeat. Repeat. Repeat six times.

Over the railing onto the track, grab the medicine ball, run, run, RUN!

"C'mon Jenny, you can do it," cried Kat from where she was cheering along the side of the track.

"Beaudean, push it now!"

It was the TAC.

"Run Jenny, Run!" yelled Kat.

I finished the first lap and dropped the medicine ball. I picked up the baton for lap number two. By the third lap my chest was screaming. As I dashed across the finish line, I prayed that my time was fast enough.

The PT instructor was an Army Captain that I knew and liked. He looked up at me from his clipboard.

"Cadet Beaudean, nice job, you earned yourself a C+," he commented as he wrote down my time.

"Great job Jenny!" said Kat with a grin and a pat on the back.

My relief was palpable. A C+! I had hoped for a C and the plus made it even better. The IOCT was a tough test. There would be other cadets who would not be so lucky. They would fail the shelf or the rope climb and in all likelihood the failure of one obstacle would mean failing the course. And failing the course jeopardized their future at the Academy. The trick to the IOCT was getting every obstacle accomplished, and getting it the first time.

I smiled. It was over. I had passed. Then my gaze shifted and I saw the TAC. He didn't look so pleased.

"Cadet Beaudean, I understand you only got a C on the Course," he said, walking toward me. He was running his fingers along the edge of his Class A trousers, making the pressed shirt look even more pressed.

"Sir, it was a C *plus*," I replied with a hint of indignation.

But instinctively I knew what was coming next.

"It's not a bad score, but I think you could do better. I think you would move a little bit faster on a course like this if you took off a little more weight."

"Yes Sir," I replied.

I joined Kat outside the gym and we walked back to the barracks in silence. I coughed. With four thousand cadets completing the obstacle course, the fibers in the ropes began to come free, and before long the old gym was a haze of fibers and dust. The "IOCT hack." My classmates and I would cough for days.

"Jenny, don't be discouraged. The man's an ass," Kat said as we walked through the door. She climbed up and reached into the hiding spot.

"Let's drown our sorrow."

With spring came 500th Night, the formal dinner and dance for the cows held to celebrate the milestone of only 500 remaining days until graduation. There was the usual parade of civilian dates in long dresses with their hair pinned up on the tops of their heads. But I hardly noticed the girls milling about outside the barracks. I had my own fish to fry. As Kat and I got ready for the 500th Night dinner, I looked unhappily at the fit of my formal Dress Mess.

Dress Mess is a striking uniform. Its long black skirt and white jacket are handsome, even with the ridiculous little tie worn at the neck.

If only the damn thing fit.

The skirt looked reasonably okay. But my stomach pooched out despite the super-control top pantyhose I had squeezed into. The jacket wouldn't close. Thank God the regulations didn't require it to be buttoned. I put on the highest black heels I owned, hoping some height would help the situation. When nothing more could be done except to suck in my stomach as much as possible, Kat and I walked down the hall to stand in front of the mirror.

I looked at what I saw with dismay. Gone was my firm and fit body of the summer before. I was back where I started.

That evening I walked up the stone steps to Boodlers and, looking around to make sure that none of my classmates were watching, bought a pint of ice cream and chips and cookies -- all of the things I had been denying myself for weeks. The food would make the ache go away. It would be a companion and friend. It would fill the emptiness.

I ate everything in the bag down to the last crumb of cookie, drowning my depression with binging. The eating was mindless and the minute the last cookie was gone, I rolled up the evidence in a little paper bag and hid it under some papers in the trash can.

But now ... I began to panic. It wouldn't be long before there was another weigh in. And right now only one pair of my ME Trou fit well. I had just eaten about 4000 calories. I couldn't possibly work off all those calories with a quick run to Thayer Gate.

The events of my life began to swirl around me -- comments from Aunt Birdie on a day long ago, starving to get ready for R Day, the hideous weight program, Matt Bailey and his never ending quest for perfection, the TAC's comment after the IOCT, Air Assault School, struggling to fit into my dress mess uniform. My entire value as a human being was clearly directly related to whether I was thin.

And worse, I had just sabotaged myself by binging on junk food.

It was like I had just jumped from the top of a building and now, on the way down, was regretting it.

All those cookies ...

I've got to get rid of it.

Without another thought except the need to get rid of the food, I went into the bathroom. When I was sure that the latrine was empty, I locked myself in the first stall, bent over the toilet and stuck my finger down my throat.

At first it was difficult to get the food to come up, but after a few tries I got the hang of it. I watched the pieces of cookies and goops of ice cream swirl around in the toilet. When my stomach was empty I flushed twice to get rid of the evidence, washed out my mouth and used soap on my hands. The toilet was clean, my hands were clean, my mouth was clean. It was as if the events of the last few minutes had never happened.

It had been much easier, if more disgusting, than I had envisioned. I felt enormously better. I had gotten rid of it all. And no one ever had to know. My stomach felt empty and flat and I ran my hand over it with glee. I was back in control of my body and my life.

I would be thin. And I didn't care anymore what it took.

The next morning I stepped on the scale. Three pounds less.

Yes!

And with that, a new friend was born.

18

"D u bist dran," he said, which in German means "It's your turn."

I looked up in confusion from where I was lying prone on the firing line.

The German NCO switched to English.

"You must pull za rifle haader into your shoulder," he continued. He reached down and pulled the rifle back against my upper arm.

I looked down range and, at the word "go," shot at the paper target.

My summer assignment between cow and firstie year took me to Berlin. It was 1990, the summer after the Wall came down. I was assigned to the 287th MP Company[37] as a part of a cadet program called CTLT. The program sent firsties out into the Army to take on the role of a platoon leader in an existing military unit. Generally the actual platoon leader would step aside for the five or six weeks to allow the cadet to practice organizing, training and leading soldiers. In a sense it was an internship and it was our first try at leading troops in the regular Army.

There was no better time to be in Berlin. The Berlin Wall, the concrete symbol of the Cold War, had come down the November before. For forty years the separation between East and West had been impregnable. Now it lay quiet with pieces chopped out of it and holes for the newly freed East Germans to pass through. Street vendors sold pieces of it as memorabilia. The "death strip," where some had died trying to cross from East to West, previously armed with mines,

---

[37] A military police unit.

dogs and guard towers, was now peaceful and deserted. Checkpoint Charlie[38] was simply a booth standing in the middle of a road. The feeling in the city was one of hope and optimism.

I looked up at the German instructor while he looked at my paper target, which he held in his hand. The little holes where my rounds had penetrated were in a reasonably tight group but there were still a few that had missed the mark.

"Das ist gut Cadet," he said with a smile, "I sink you huv to *focus* more so za shots meet za center of za target."

"Yes, I'll do that, thank you Sergeant," I replied.

He was right. I was focused on other things – like how to get rid of lunch.

I excused myself and found a latrine that was quiet and out of the way. Checking to make sure the other stalls were empty, I quickly shut the door and bent over the toilet.

The "quick fix" on 500th night was now a daily event and a new psychology was forming. At times I sat down to a meal with no intention of purging afterward, but if I took one bite too many and ended the meal feeling too full, I felt a sense of panic and was compelled to get rid of the food. For the first time I felt in complete control of my weight and no one was the wiser. At a nice, neat 138 pounds, I was running hard every morning and throwing up in the afternoon, all with the belief shared by the young that my body was invincible and would somehow survive the mistreatment.

Anything to be thin.

Back at the Academy in the fall, my new friend became a constant companion as football season ramped up. Tailgates were full of chips, burgers, ice cream and brownies, and the ability to purge gave me the latitude to eat anything I liked. I

---

[38] During the Cold War and while the Berlin Wall stood, Checkpoint Charlie was manned by American, British and French military and was the single passage point between East Berlin and West Berlin. It existed for 27 years before the Wall fell.

became an expert on every bathroom on post – where they were located, when they were unlocked, when they were deserted. Now the bulimia was not only my savior, it had its own process and rhythm.

> *Hungry. Haven't eaten yet today.*
> *Ice cream, chips, cookies.*
> *Feeling full ... too full.*
> *Excuse myself with a pleasant word.*
> *Find the safest latrine. No one is around.*
> *Bend over the toilet, index and second finger down the throat.*
> *Out it all comes.*
> *Flush. Twice.*
> *Wash hands well. Rinse out mouth.*
> *Dab eyes where tears have formed.*
> *Rejoin the party.*
> *Still in control of my body.*

As I nurtured and befriended my eating disorder I began to notice the habits of other female cadets. There were others like me -- female cadets who took long trips to the bathroom and emerged with watery, puffy eyes. There were those who pushed their food around their plates, eating little more than a bite or two. Some female cadets exercised three times per day. It seemed apparent that there were other young women at West Point who had secrets -- an obsession with exercising, issues with body image, bulimia, anorexia or all of the above.

On the night in October when I was assigned as Staff Duty Officer, the Captain who was the Officer in Charge looked up and down my uniform and nodded his head in approval. The assignment of Staff Duty Officer rotated between the thousand firsties in my class. I would spend the night walking through the barracks and making my inspections. If I was lucky, I'd catch an hour or two of sleep in Central Guard Room.

I walked out for my first inspection of the night and paused in the sallyport to look across the Plain. It was my favorite time of year at West Point. The green of the Plain was deep and lush, the sun was setting and the sky was pink, all set off by the orange and deep scarlet leaves that ran up the sides of the Hudson.

I still can't believe I'm here.

Despite the long night ahead I was in a good mood. For once I was out of trouble. Classes were going well. I had just passed my physical fitness test with a respectable A- and I hadn't walked the Area in ages. Most of all, my stomach was flat, my weight was 137 pounds. That was all that mattered. My bulimia had become a daily event but I welcomed my thinner self regardless of the cost and reveled in the way my trousers sat on my waist.

It was near midnight as I walked across the Area to Grant Barracks, where my company lived, to drop in on Kat. I looked up to see the stars above my head.

All seemed well with the world.

The second I opened the door to the Barracks, I knew that it was not. It was loud -- too loud. Half on the stoops, half inside, I stood in the doorway and hesitated. I already knew the truth -- my roommate was drunk and there were others with her. On any other night I would have been sharing in the secret stash of vodka. But as the SDO, I was duty-bound to report any infraction, regardless of who might be involved. The mantra of the Academy was not "Duty, Honor, Country, but not if it involves your roommate."

Kat poked her head out the door and we exchanged a long look.

"Jenny," started Kat, half gasping, half laughing.

I held up my hand and turned to go.

As the cadet in charge, I was obligated to investigate and write Kat and the others up for drinking in the barracks. But in the hours that waned toward dawn, the window of opportunity closed for me to do my duty. As first light seeped through the window I knew I didn't have the strength to report my friend. So I took a tremendous gamble that it would all dispel quietly, that no one would ever be the wiser, that there would be no need to ever discuss it.

Maybe no one would find out.

But they did.

The door swung open and Major Devlin, the TAC, looked at me darkly. His office was immaculate. His life was about military order. I was a wrinkle in that neatly pressed world.

"Cadet Beaudean, get in here!"

I took a few steps forward, executed a left face and stood at the position of attention in front of his desk. I saluted.

"Sir, Cadet Beaudean reports as ordered."

The drum beat out on the Plain and I could hear it through his open window. Soon the Hellcats would play the first note of the march. Cadet feet would step in unison across the Plain. For once I desperately wished to be on the parade field.

"What happened?" the TAC asked, looking up from the folder.

I wanted to pee.

"Did you *know* they were drinking?" he continued, "Did you see the alcohol?"

"No Sir."

"But you *thought* they were drinking," he said.

"Yes Sir," I replied truthfully.

"Then it's sort of irrelevant whether they were or weren't," he said softly, "because you suspected that there was drinking in the barracks and yet you didn't follow through. You didn't do your duty. It's inexcusable."

"Yes Sir."

The drum sounded again. *Thunk, thunk, thunk.*

"Cadet Beaudean, this is why we call it *duty.* They're your friends but they're in the wrong. You are in *charge* as the officer on duty, and so you *do* your duty and you *report* them! You'll walk the area for your lapse in judgment. Graduation is not too far away. I'd better not see your face again during the next six months. Your uniform will be straight," his voice rose, "your room will be flawless, your grades will be good — is that clear?"

"Yes Sir! Sir, may I ask a question," I asked bravely.

"What?" the TAC replied impatiently.

"Sir, what will happen to Cadet McNeil?"

He looked away. Now he was the one who looked uncomfortable.

"Nothing will happen to Cadet McNeil. While we know by your own admission that you felt they were drinking but ignored your duty to investigate and report the infraction, we have no proof that she in fact was taking a drink."

I lost my patience and my wisdom in the same breath.

"So Sir, *they* were drinking in the barracks but *I'm* going to walk the Area."

The TAC put his hands on his desk, leaned across it and looked me in the eye.

"Cadet Beaudean, you'd better do an about face and get out of my office right now."

As we dressed for dinner that night, Kat pinned her hair in front of the mirror without a word. The room was silent and uncomfortable. I wiped off my saber and put it in its place on my waist. I looked at my roommate, the picture of perfection in front of the glass.

Kat did not say a word in my defense in the weeks following my night on SDO. There was no brilliant show of heroism on the part of my roommate, no dash to rescue her friend, no show of solidarity. What sense would it have made for us both to serve Area tours? But there was also no apology.

Two weeks later I walked out to the Area. I could see Kat in the window laughing with a would-be suitor as she held the curling iron to her hair. She looked beautiful and ready for an evening out.

I turned and walked to Central Area and took my place in formation.

"In some ways I think it was the best thing that God made your looks secondary," my father said one afternoon as we caught up by phone.

I looked out at the plebes doing pushups in the sinks and thought about his comment.

What does one say to a statement like that? Thank you?

"Dad, I could have stood with a little bit more in the looks department," I replied.

"I know it feels that way," he continued, "But there will be plenty of time in your life to wear beautiful clothes and do your hair and go out on dates. For your time at West Point you needed to concentrate -- concentrate on what matters! You may not have had a lot of male attention but in a way it was the best thing – you weren't distracted – and now you're about to win the prize you've worked so hard for ... Graduation is right around the corner!"

I understood what he was saying.

But if God had been handing out looks like Audrey Hepburn the day I was born I would have gladly signed up.

When January came and with it second semester, I was assigned as the Battalion Supply Officer for 2nd Battalion, 1st Regiment. The new assignment meant leaving my company area in Grant Barracks, moving to a different part of the Corps with a new roommate.

Pershing Barracks was one of the oldest buildings in the cadet area and rumored to have a ghost. As I pulled my footlocker up the flight of stairs to the second floor I took a look around. The building was old, with beautiful wide hallways and high ceilings -- but there was nothing unusual in sight.

A classmate looked out the doorway of one of the rooms.

"You lookin' for the ghost? You can only hear him at night."

"Uh huh," I replied with skepticism.

I didn't care.

I gladly welcomed the paranormal if it meant leaving my merciless classmates and the drama of living with Kat.

The move and the new assignment were a tremendous stroke of luck. I was now away from the distraction of the never-ending male suitors lined up to see my roommate. The company mates who had teased me constantly over the four years were now an Area away. I rarely encountered Major Devlin and the tone and daily interaction on battalion staff was professional and positive. For the first time, life as a cadet was genuinely pleasant.

As for my friendship with Kat, I hardly saw her.

On my last afternoon serving Area tours I had a friend take a photo of me in front of the sign "Area tours in progress" and sent it to my father with a note. He laughed and responded with a single line, "You're on the home stretch now. Stay out of trouble!"

There it was, in sight now.

The prize – just a stone's throw away.

Graduation was so close I could taste it.

19

The first of June, 1991 -- Graduation Day. My graduating class was the busiest we had been since plebe year. There were final exams to take but the tests were only a small part of the picture. We were caught up in the all-consuming preparation to take our first active duty assignment as brand new second lieutenants.

First class cadets were assigned to an Army branch and a duty station based on class rank. My rank was respectable, in the middle of the class, but it was certainly not high enough to get my first choice, Military Police, or a duty station like Hawaii. I did get my second choice for branch, the Army Corps of Engineers, but practically no choice for my duty station. I was assigned to the 43rd Engineer Battalion at Fort Benning, Georgia.

"What's in Georgia?" asked my mother over the phone a few nights before the big day. I could hear her smacking the sheets as she folded the laundry.

"I don't know," I replied, "Army Airborne School, the home of the Infantry, and apparently the 43rd Engineer Battalion."

"I have a feeling that our wonderful New York City will seem far away but who knows, maybe they have museums or something."

You had to love my mother's optimism.

Many Army posts are in the middle of nowhere surrounded by tattoo parlors, strip clubs, dry cleaners, car dealerships and pawnshops.

The days were long as we packed our gear and were fitted for our new green Army uniforms. The Army skirt I would wear as a part of my Dress A uniform looked awful despite several fittings, so I dragged my sewing machine out of the storage locker in the basement and set up shop on the desk in my room. I carefully ripped out the seams and refashioned the shape. I was determined to look smashing for the bar pinning ceremony after graduation.

141 pounds.

The tasks were never-ending. We stenciled our names and new unit on our Army footlockers and sorted through four years' worth of equipment. We reported at the appointed hour to receive our official Army orders to join our new units. I even had to make an appearance in a room in Washington Hall to record the correct pronunciation of my name so that it would be announced properly during graduation.

And what lay ahead? None of us knew. It was the spring of 1991. The first Gulf War had kicked off and ended in under a week. But the future was uncertain and I wondered if a deployment to the Middle East lay ahead.

Five days before graduation.

The minute I saw David Donnally waiting by the edge of Lusk Reservoir with piles of scuba gear and realized he would be testing my group for my scuba certification, I knew it would be a long afternoon.

With only a few hours of sleep per night, a schedule and demands that were relentless, the last thing I needed was to don a wetsuit for scuba certification. But West Point doesn't really factor your level of mental exhaustion into how it times its events. So I dutifully showed up at the bank of the Reservoir on the appointed afternoon.

David was a classmate and a Regimental Commander. He was blond, blue-eyed, broad-chested and very "enthusiastic" about rules and regulations. He was a military overachiever, so much so that his actions often prompted jeers from the cadets who were forced to do his bidding. He also was an experienced diver.

"Think positively," I told myself with determination and pulled on my wet suit.

My group swam away from the shore, descended to ten feet, and followed David under water to the middle of the reservoir.

Two hours later my cheerful determination had diminished substantially. David was a strong swimmer and easily covered long distances with my male classmates right behind him. I was working hard to keep up, with my little fins going like crazy under the water. My thighs burned and I huffed and puffed through the regulator. As I brought up the rear there were looks of impatience.

Once again my athletic ability was the bane of my existence.

"Let's get the guys certified first," David said to me, "and then we can finish up."

An hour later the guys were done and I was alone with David, still swimming furiously to finish the test. With one task to go, David checked my air supply.

"Hmm, you're going to need another tank," he mused.

My face fell.

"You've got to be kidding me," I panted in dismay, "There's only one task to go!"

"There's another tank on shore," David replied, disregarding my comment and waving toward the bank.

I looked back to where the extra tank rested far across the water. All of my male classmates were sitting on the shore – watching me.

Is that beer they're drinking?

David took off for shore without another word and I had no choice but to follow, cursing him silently as we went.

As I clamored up the bank in my fins, face red with exertion, I faced the sad reality that I must look like a bulbous penguin with a beet for a face. I tried to look dignified as two of the guys helped David strap the new tank onto my back.

"Okay, we're all set," said David cheerfully, and made for the water.

I waddled after him, working hard not to trip over my fins.

By some miracle, I completed certification an hour later.

One more box checked.

Finally, the big day arrived.

The alarm went off at 0530 and, with only an hour's sleep under my belt, I swung my legs over the side of the bed and made my way to the latrine. I leaned against the wall in the shower and let the hot water pour over me, hoping to cure my aching head.

Then, as I did every morning, I stepped on the scale.

The day I graduated West Point I weighed 144 pounds.

Traditionally the graduating class wears the full dress coat with its signature brass buttons over white slacks for the graduation ceremony. But we had worn that uniform the day before for the Graduation Parade and, as the Hellcats played and we marched on the Plain for the last time, the skies opened up with a deluge of rain. We were soaked to the skin. The legend goes that a graduating class that gets rained on during the Parade will go to war. And, as I write this, a classmate of mine is in Iraq for the *fourth* time and so I think we can say that, for my class at least, the legend held true.

The cadet laundry's answer to the soaking wet full dress coats was to attempt to dry them overnight in preparation for the graduation ceremony. The coats came back the next morning shrunken, misshapen, with buttons missing from their trip through the dryer and it was quickly decided that our class would instead graduate in the magnificent all-white India White uniform.

"We'd better go," my roommate said.

We were adjusting each other's red sash and as she tugged at mine I looked around the room. Much of the cadet trappings were packed and on their way to storage or our duty station. The smell in the barracks was the same. Voices of the underclassman sounded in the halls and outside on the Area. And I knew that West Point would march on without even missing us. The pulse and tradition would not miss a beat upon our departure.

As we passed by the hallway mirror I looked critically at my body, just as I had countless times per day since I was a plebe. But excitement of the day soon took over my thoughts. The door slammed behind us, and my roommate and I walked up the steps of the Cadet Chapel, winding our way up to Michie Stadium with the rest of our classmates in a long trail of white uniforms. Two hours later we stepped off in a stadium full of family and friends and marched across the field. I could see President Bush out of the corner of my eye and wondered where in the bleachers my parents were sitting.

The National Anthem played and my eyes filled with tears. I blotted them with the edge of my white glove and spots of mascara speckled the cloth. Speeches were made and people were recognized. Then my name was called. I stepped in front of the President of the United States and raised my right hand in a sharp salute.

President Bush handed me my diploma, shook my hand and smiled at me.

"Way to go Lieutenant."

"Thank you Sir," I replied and walked past him and down the steps of the stage.

Before I knew it, we were raising our right hands to repeat the oath and accept our commissions. We declared our loyalty to our nation and our commitment to fight any enemy that threatened its freedom.

"I love my America," I thought and took the oath without hesitation.

There was quiet across the stadium as the Brigade Commander received his orders to dismiss the class.

Executing a perfect about face, he hollered, "Class DISMISSED!"

Whoosh!

With all of my might I threw my white hat above my head and watched it flip in the air above me.

"Thank you Lord," I whispered.

It was over.

The psychologist looked at me over her notes.

"When you look back, what was the best day of your life?"

"Graduation Day," I replied without missing a beat, "That was the best day of my life. The best *moment* of my life was the moment when we threw our hats in the air."

"Most people say that the best day of their life was their wedding day or the day a child was born," she commented.

"*Hands down*, Graduation Day was the best day," I replied with conviction.

"Were you bulimic all during that time?" she asked.

"Yes," I replied, "Every day ... sometimes twice."

"And yet despite your eating disorder, this was the best day."

"It took *everything* I had to get through those four years. *Everything.*"

"So you weren't thinking about your bulimia," she said.

"Not at all. By that time, it was just a way of life."

Brand new second lieutenants on either side of me were hugging each other and the people they loved. My family made their way toward me amidst the children dashing across the field to pick up the white hats. In a rush my father came to me and scooped me up.

"I did it Dad," I whispered into his shoulder.

"I know," he choked, "it's over now and you're victorious."

We stood on the field holding each other.

"You're a brand new second lieutenant," he smiled.

"Yes Sir," I replied with a grin.

The rest of the afternoon was filled with goodbyes to classmates, final turn-in of gear and the bar pinning ceremony. I donned my new Army green Class A uniform. Standing on the lawn next to the Cadet Chapel, my mother stood on one side and my grandmother on the other. They pinned on the new rank of 2nd Lieutenant.

Finally we made for home. My mother had planned a surprise party for me and the house was filled with family and friends. There were hugs and congratulations, accolades and handshakes. I was grateful to my family for all of their support and presented them with the saber I had carried as a firstie. As the last guest waved good-bye we stood together in the same kitchen where I had eaten my solitary egg for breakfast on R Day. I helped my mother put the last of the dishes away and the house became quiet as I went to my room.

It was finished … finally.

Then I went to bed and slept for three days.

20

S tand UP!"
The jumpmaster was standing in the rear of the aircraft and he looked down the line at the students of my Airborne class. We were seated side by side, packed in like sardines. The roar of the plane made it nearly impossible to be heard, but the jumpmaster managed to break through the din with his instructions. With his directive to stand up, we rose in unison, executed a right face and faced the tail of the plane.

"Hook UP!"

A long cable ran along the middle of the C130 and we reached up and clipped our static lines[39] to the cable, making sure the clips were closed. Once we left the door of the aircraft, the static line would grab hold and pull the parachute out of the pack on each of our backs.

The engines slowed as we approached the drop zone and the jumpmaster opened the door at the rear of the aircraft to a roar of engines and wind.

"Stand IN the door!" the jumpmaster called.

The second lieutenant in charge of the 2nd Stick moved into position. Gripping the sides of the opening, he braced himself to jump.

"Here we go!" yelled the sergeant behind me.

I only nodded.

Jump number four. We had three jumps under our belts, but leaping from a perfectly good airplane was still just this side of nuts.

---

[39] A static line pulls the parachute out of its case as the soldier exits the plane.

The traffic light hanging at the back of the plane suddenly turned green.

"GO! GO! GO! GO!" the jumpmaster hollered.

With the lieutenant from 2nd Stick in the lead, we pushed each other out the door in as tight a group as possible. The second I left the plane I was sucked into the rush of wind. As the C130 pulled away the static line jerked and caught, pulling my chute from its pack. I looked up. Sailing happily above me was a green Army parachute, the Dash 1 Bravo, big and round.

With the parachute over my head, I had a moment to enjoy the view. The only sound was the wind. The tree line that bordered the drop zone was small and distant. There were dozens of soldiers with parachutes overhead sailing beside me in either direction as far as the eye could see.

I looked down. The ground was coming up.

Time to land.

It was hotter than hell in Georgia during the month of June. My Airborne class had spent the last three weeks soaked with sweat, our days filled with P.T. at 0400 hours, NCOs yelling at us basic-training-style and "good Army training." The bulk of the classes took place in enormous pits of woodchips where we had some cushion as we learned to land. As we jumped from towers and wood stands, learning to roll as our feet hit the ground, we were covered in the little chips, which made their way into every crack and crevice of our uniforms and bodies.

The training was all about the landing.

After all, falling isn't particularly difficult.

Army parachutes are designed to get a soldier to the ground as quickly as possible with the rationale that the longer she or he floats above the earth, the more likely the enemy can take a shot. Landings are a controlled crash. Despite the Airborne training of "feet and knees together" for a safe landing, I had done a "feet, knees, face" the previous day on Jump #3, and came up for air with sand in my teeth.

We jumped with a main parachute on our backs, a suspiciously small reserve on our abdomens and, for some jumps, rucksacks strung beneath the reserve and our rifles in a case at our side. Each jump began with a trek out to the "shed" where we sat on long wooden tables until the jump zone was ready and the C130 was cleared for takeoff. The tables weren't terribly high off the ground, but the gear was cumbersome and I am reasonably short. My predicament brought grins from the good-natured soldiers in my stick. Without a word, two of them would stand on either side of me, lifting me up to sit on the table.

It was all about teamwork.

Hours later, when clearance came for us to go, I was so hot, my parachute harness was so tight and I had to pee so badly that I was ready to jump out of the plane just to get to the nearest latrine.

"Let's GO!" called the jumpmaster.

The School was nearly finished. Airborne wings required five successful jumps to receive the badge. One jump to go and I'd have my wings. I would *finally* have a badge on my uniform. Victory was so close I could taste it.

I looked down.

The ground was coming up fast. Rocks were visible, and grass.

I pressed my feet and knees together as hard as I could and looked out at the horizon as I had been trained so as not to anticipate my feet hitting the ground.

But at the last second ... the wind picked up.

Dazed, I looked at the blue sky over my head. I was in an odd position but I picked my head up to look at my feet. My left boot was askew, my lower leg at an odd angle.

Suddenly a face appeared above mine.

"We saw you come in Lieutenant. What happened?"

"Not sure Sir," I replied, a little disoriented.

"You hit the ground hard. Were you running with the wind?"

What?

I didn't answer, still disoriented and still looking at my leg, which lay useless on the ground. The lieutenant colonel, however, appeared determined to get an answer and queried me again.

"Do you think your chute malfunctioned?"

I looked at him with frustration.

*Are we going to have this conversation **right now**?*

"Sir, I think it's broken."

The colonel must have decided that we could decipher the ins and outs of my fourth landing at a later date and he disappeared to call for the ambulance. My head dropped back. The blue sky above me had writing all over it and I recognized every word. There would be no jump number five. There would be no Airborne wings. I knew what was ahead -- surgery, crutches, physical therapy -- months of recovery without the ability to run and exercise.

The mounting pain in my leg was trumped by the worst thought of all.

What would the lack of exercise mean for my weight?

139 pounds.

Days later I lay in the hospital. My leg and ankle were swollen to twice their normal size. Surgery was delayed for two weeks while my leg was packed in ice. I had broken the fibula in half and a nice sized chunk from the end of my tibia, and torn all the ligaments down the middle.

"So I need the hospital food daily total to equal 1200 calories," I continued.

The hospital dietician nodded.

"No problem Lieutenant, we'll make sure you don't gain weight while you can't exercise."

"Thank you Ma'am," I replied in relief.

Got to keep the priorities straight. Hard to be bulimic on crutches.

I looked up to see a figure in the doorway. It was my classmate, Christopher Mason. As the dietician left, he took my hand and kissed away my tears.

Christopher and I had met shortly before graduation and our "dating" initially consisted of evening runs out to Lee Gate and back. He was the roommate of a good friend and we became running buddies mostly out of convenience – our schedules matched. Christopher was tall and handsome, with sandy brown hair, blue eyes and a radiant smile. And he was a soldier at heart. He was the kind of soldier that military leaders dream of – squared away, tactically proficient, a great strategist and a good leader to boot. He was just like Matt Bailey – military life for him was a natural fit. And despite my reservations about getting involved with a guy who was an ultra-whooah, strack cadet who branched Infantry, I warmed to his genuine nature. Before long a friendship had formed.

One thing led to another and, by the morning of our graduation, I was smitten.

He sat next to me on the hospital bed and spoon fed me jello.

"It's gonna be okay," he told me with confidence, "Try not to worry."

Maybe it was the drama of the moment – me in a hospital bed with my prince at my side. Maybe it was the fact that the Army would only station us together if we were married. Maybe it was the prescription painkillers. Whatever it was, I knew at that moment that he would be my husband. He was everything I had ever wanted. He was my father and Matt Bailey rolled into one. I didn't want to live another minute without him.

My recovery took nearly six months. The first surgery pieced my leg together with a plate and seven screws in the bones, and an eighth, longer screw through both bones to pull the ankle joint back together so the ligaments could heal. The second surgery, two months later, removed the longest screw so I could walk again.

Christopher and I fell in love that fall as I fought my way through physical therapy, an infection in the incision and ten weeks on crutches while he attended the Infantry Officer Basic Course, which is also located at Fort Benning. Once my stitches were removed, I became a fixture at the gymnasium pool. I stood on one leg in the locker room, changed into my bathing suit, and then "crab walked," sliding on my bottom to the edge of the pool, where I would plop into the water to swim laps.

Anything to stay thin.

I learned how to prop myself on one foot in the bathroom while I purged "one bite too many" from dinner or a pint of Ben & Jerry's ice cream or pancakes from a big breakfast at the local diner. Christopher was none the wiser.

One night in his room at the B.O.Q.[40] the phone rang.

And my world changed.

"So it's not a pinched nerve," I said.

"No," my father responded quietly, "Hang on, your mother's going to get on."

"Why is my mother getting on?" I asked.

The phone clicked as my mother picked up the extension.

"What is it?" I asked.

"They think its A.L.S.," my father said, "... Lou Gehrig's Disease."

Silence. I had seen the movie about Lou Gehrig.

"Isn't that terminal?" I asked after a long pause.

"It can be," my father replied.

"What do you mean it *can* be?"

Suddenly I was angry with him. How dare he be sick? How dare any part of the world threaten his existence? And how dare he not be *angry* about it?

"There's reason to be hopeful," my father went on, "The disease progresses differently for each person and sometimes even stops entirely."

---

[40] Bachelor Officers Quarters.

"So we're going to hope for that," said my mother with forced enthusiasm.

ALS, or Amyotrophic Lateral Sclerosis, is a neurological degenerative disease that attacks nerve cells in the brain and spinal cord. As the disease progresses, the motor neurons in the body start to die and the patient begins a process of slow paralysis, losing the ability to move their limbs. Eventually the paralysis can affect speech, swallowing and breathing. The disease has no affect on cognitive ability, so the patient is usually functioning mentally but trapped in their body, unable to move or function. ALS is often called Lou Gehrig's disease, named for the famous baseball Hall of Famer who played for the New York Yankees and was diagnosed in 1939.

He died two years later.

21

January 1992.

The snow fell outside my BOQ window at Fort Leonard Wood, Missouri, home of the US Army Corps of Engineers where I was assigned to complete the Officer Basic Course. The schooling was a preliminary and branch-related training to ready new lieutenants to take over their platoons. In its simplest form, the mission of the Corps of Engineers was to build things or blow them up. I would spend the next six months learning how to build structures, roads and bridges while also learning how to use every explosive device imaginable to turn them into sawdust.

Christopher accompanied me to Missouri to help me get settled. We spent a few days unpacking my clothes and my gear. Christopher spit-shined my boots while I ironed my shirts. I smiled at him from across the room and he winked at me. I looked at the lines on his face and the spot where he had cut himself shaving. At that moment I wished for us to never be apart.

He crossed the room and put his arms around me, "Soon we'll be together forever." I touched his eyebrows and ran my hand along his face.

"I don't want you to go," I replied with my cheek on his chest.

"This is just a blade of grass. If our life together is a big field, the time that we're apart is only a blade of grass," he said and he kissed me.

The next day Christopher left to drive back to Fort Benning where he would complete additional coursework and Ranger School.

And so began the love letters.

The first one I found tucked under my pillow the night he drove away.

He wrote that he would gladly miss me versus having someone else. He said he loved me. He couldn't wait for me to be his wife.

My letters to him were equally impassioned. My world seemed empty when he was gone and I couldn't wait to start our life together. It was a Romeo & Juliet kind of love, the kind of devotion where I felt that I could hardly take a breath if he wasn't in my world. Sometimes I wrote to him two or three times during the day, finding minutes in between classes to jot a note and send my thoughts to him. And nearly every day his replies would greet me in my mailbox.

When I wasn't thinking of Christopher I was thinking of my father.

By the time I arrived at Fort Leonard Wood, his illness was well underway. He shuffled now when he walked, dragging his left leg. His left arm was mostly useless. The congregation at the Lutheran church where my father was pastor adored him and quickly built wheelchair ramps and other modifications to make it possible for him to continue serving. But it was obvious that the disease was progressing, each day a bit more strength lost, a little more freedom relinquished.

With my dad sick and Christopher gone I was beside myself with worry. Hoping that a busy schedule would provide a cure for my growing depression, I volunteered for the position of company first sergeant. Professionally it was a smart move. The leadership skills I had honed at Camp Buckner and in Berlin blossomed and my performance met with good reviews.

But a perfect storm of misery was taking hold.

One night on the phone I noticed the change in my father's voice. His words were starting to slur.

"What's happening?" I asked my mother, "Why doesn't he sound the same?"

"The A.L.S. is affecting his tongue now so he can't formulate words like he used to."

The phone was silent on her end and on mine as we both cried.

He's getting sicker.

And as my father got sicker, I got sicker.

My bulimia was my daily companion, binging at night to try to fill the emptiness, purging right after to try and make the pain go away.

"Do you blame God?" I asked him.

I had been granted a weekend pass and was home with my family.

I put together another forkful of rice and chicken and held it up for him to take in his mouth. As he swallowed, he coughed a little. The A.L.S. was affecting everything now. He was having difficulty swallowing.

"No," he said, shaking his head, "I don't blame God."

"Maybe I'll just blame God for both of us." I said.

I looked at his hands and his arms thin with atrophy and I hated God for allowing a man with such faith to suffer so.

"Don't blame God," my father said with a note of passion, "This is the way life is. Sometimes it's just luck of the draw. I just happened to be the one who got this disease. I don't know the plan, but I believe that He has one."

I put my hand on his arm.

"Dad," I choked and said in a whisper, "If you die, I hope that wherever you are, God lets you kind of 'look in' sometimes, y'know?"

I caught my breath and continued.

"I hope He'll let you see how we are and what we're doing. I hope you can still be with us, with me. I don't know how to be in a world where you aren't."

He smiled at me and tried to raise his hand to take mine ... then realized again that he couldn't.

144.

June 20, 1992

Our wedding day dawned bright and sunny. It seemed a natural choice for Christopher and I to get married at West Point and so we made our way back to the Academy for the big day.

My father's illness was costing the family a fortune so money was tight and the wedding was a mostly homemade affair. On the day of our marriage my family came together to plan out the logistics. My mother suggested that my sister stay with my father at our home in New Jersey to get my dad dressed and ready. Meanwhile my mother and I would go ahead and meet Christopher to set up one of the rooms in the basement of the Cadet Chapel for the reception. As a family we were a united front and we were consumed with keeping my father on his feet and his dignity intact.

My mother and I laid out the tablecloths and wine glasses while Christopher lugged in buckets of ice for the drinks. The day was warm and before long we were all covered in sweat. Christopher took a quick run to a friend's house for a shower and I stood in front of the large standing fan in my shorts, trying to cool off before putting on the white dress.

Aunt Birdie stood next to me as we pulled the white gown over my head.

I had been watching my weight but, once again, the number was stubborn.

The day I got married I weighed 144 pounds.

"The zipper doesn't quite want to close," said Aunt Birdie in her Midwestern lilt with ... just a hint of chiding?

My mother and I exchanged a look.

"Birdie, why don't you see if Beth has arrived with Jack," my mother suggested, sending my aunt away. Without another word she whipped out a needle and thread and sewed the cloth over the zipper where it refused to lay flat.

"There," she said with reassurance, "you're all set and you look lovely."

Fifteen minutes later I walked up the long aisle of the Cadet Chapel as the magnificent church organ filled the sanctuary. My father officiated with one of the Army chaplains and gave the sermon. And for the entire time he stood on the altar my mother, my sister and I collectively held our breath and prayed that he would remain on his feet.

"I now pronounce you husband and wife," my father said.

Christopher took my face in his hands and kissed me. For a moment I forgot about my father's illness and thought only of the man in front of me.

"Forever," I thought.

22

August 23, 1993. The voice on the phone was my sister's. "You need to come home."

The next morning I was on a plane out of Austin.

Christopher and I had arrived at Fort Hood, Texas in 1992. He would join the 1st Cavalry Division as an Infantry platoon leader and I followed my orders to join the 62nd Engineer Battalion, a heavy construction unit tasked with erecting structures, roads and bridges. By 1993, the first Gulf War was over and the Army was downsizing. As Army posts across the country were closed, excess units were moved to Fort Hood until the post was enormous and had more than 100,000 troops.

The twenty three soldiers in my platoon were a pleasure to lead, but our company commander was the devil himself. Captain William Grannis had a brilliant mind for strategy, knew weaponry like the back of his hand and spent his weekends reading about military history. But he was arrogant and childish and threw temper tantrums when his soldiers didn't live up to his expectations. Quick to blame, he berated the troops in front of their peers and his officers in front of their troops. While his technical and tactical competence was second to none, they were negated by his disregard for human decency and respect.

And it was about to come to a head.

I looked down at the clipboard where I was making notes. It was May and temperatures in central Texas easily topped 100 degrees each day. At 0600 hours, it was already warm.

The commander was hot on the heels of every platoon leader to improve vehicle maintenance for the upcoming brigade inspection. We started the day in the motorpool early, crawling under vehicles and equipment, fixing, repairing, changing fluids and filling out maintenance paperwork.

I could hear four of my soldiers talking from where they lay on their backs under a humvee. They recounted the weekend exploits, which included two of them getting lucky, one not so lucky and one tattooed. The stories were ribald and not to be believed, but who knew?

They crawled out from under the humvee to break for a cup of coffee.

Captain Grannis strode across the motorpool.

"Lieutenant Beaudean, maybe you can explain to me why your platoon is drinking coffee instead of working on vehicle maintenance!"

My soldiers heard him. I could see their faces and the sympathetic looks.

The commander stopped in front of me, his hands on his hips.

What Captain Grannis didn't count on was that his platoon leader was spoiling for a fight. I was emotionally drained and had a sense of dread about the future. My father was fully paralyzed and could not swallow, speak or hold his head up. I had not been home in months and I blamed myself for not asserting myself with the commander to get leave. I hadn't asked him for the time off – my fault. But the commander hadn't sympathized or offered support either, and most of the chain of command knew of my father's condition.

"For the love of Christ, are you going to *cry* Lieutenant?" Grannis sneered.

That was *it*.

I felt the familiar calm come over my body.

I was *done*.

I took a step toward Grannis and in no uncertain terms told him my complete and unedited opinion of his command.

I pointed out his many instances of public humiliation of his soldiers and the inappropriateness of such displays. I described the childish nature of his many temper tantrums. I reminded him of my father's illness and his lack of compassion or support. And as a parting blow I made it clear that if he ever tried to humiliate me in front of my soldiers again I would go straight to the battalion commander.

Grannis was silent, stunned.

I turned on my heel and strode away. What I had done was unthinkable. I could be relieved of my platoon. But I was at the end of my rope and as I thought about my father miles away, I didn't care.

Later I would be able to recall little about how my father's last days unfolded -- the goodbye with Christopher, lugging baggage, renting a car. Instead I remember my mother, wan and exhausted, standing in the doorway of my father's hospital room, waiting for me.

"You go in and be with him," my mother told me, putting her hand on my arm, "You tell him *everything* you want him to hear."

My father lay emaciated, a shell of the vibrant man who had once stood outside Grant Hall, eyes alight, waiting to see me, so enthused about life. He was unconscious and his glasses rested on the table. I took his hand and sat down on the edge of the bed.

Now I wasn't an Army officer or a platoon leader or a West Point grad. I was just a girl looking at the face the father she adored, knowing that what was said here and now would never be possible again. The rush of words came out in whispers and choked confessions, apologies for not being home more during his illness, professions of love for him and what he meant to me.

What lies ahead for you? Is there a heaven and will you get to look down on us sometimes and see what our lives become?

Are you proud of me?

I would never hear his voice again.

135 pounds.

In those last moments on Friday night, August 27, my mother hummed a hymn with her arms around my father's head. My sister stood on one side, holding his left hand, while I stood on the other, holding his right. My grandmother stood at his feet.

The heart monitor slowed and he began to slip away.

I whispered my last words to him with desperation.

"Oh *Dad* ... I wish you didn't have to *go*."

With a few last few beats, his heart stopped. There was no fanfare, no noise -- no fight in him to continue living. His death was not violent or painful.

Outside, I looked up at the sky. There were bright stars out and I could hear music from a car in the parking lot.

Life went on, didn't miss a beat.

My mother, my sister and I began the endless preparations to send the dead to rest. There were countless people to call, too many tasks to number.

I stood beside my mother four days later at the grave site and held her hand. My sister was on her other side, doing the same. As the casket was lowered, the words of the minister faded away and I was lost in memories -- my father pushing me on my bicycle, my father discussing politics in the kitchen, my father stirring the huge vat in which he made homemade wine.

Suddenly I was back in the laundry room the day before I reported to West Point. He was standing in front of the dryer, his back to me. That was the day before R Day.

I started to say something to him and then realized that he was weeping, his shoulders shaking with emotion. He took me in his arms tightly, sobbing.

"You have to make your own life now," he wept as he held me.

I nodded and held him back, weeping myself.

It was the only time in my life that I saw my father cry.

I returned to Fort Hood three weeks later. My father's absence surfaced at odd, unexpected moments – while wrapping Christmas gifts, hearing a song I knew he loved, or stirring a pot of oatmeal reminiscent of his "Oatmeal Royale." I did everything I could to pour myself into the life that my husband and I were building. "Nesting," my mother called it. I tucked away the grief and loss so that I could concentrate on my professional life and my marriage.

But neither was meant to last.

To his credit, Captain Grannis never spoke of the incident in the motorpool and seemed to realize that he and the circumstances had pushed me over the edge. His leadership style never changed, but his interactions with me and my soldiers were improved in the following months. I moved on with a solid performance review from him and became a battalion staff officer.

Meanwhile my bulimia took on a life of its own.

Sometimes it was quiet, dormant, disappearing for months at a time.

Where have you gone my friend?

Then it would surface again, stronger than ever, demanding my attention on a daily basis, sometimes twice a day.

Anything to be thin.

The broken ankle I sustained at Airborne School was never quite the same and it interfered with my ability to do my job. In 1994, the Army and I agreed that it was time to call it quits. Through a Medical Board, I was honorably discharged and I began my career in business. Then in 1997, Christopher's successful entrée into federal law enforcement took us to Detroit, Michigan.

And then things began to unravel in earnest.

137 pounds.

23

April 2000.
"Shhhhh," my sister laughed, "We're gonna keep everybody up!"

"By everybody, you mean Richard," replied my mother referring to my sister's husband who was trying to sleep on the other side of the wall.

As if in response, Richard gave us three knocks from the other side of the wall in agreement.

Our response was stifled giggles.

Christopher and I were living in Michigan, where his job had taken us. The rest of my family lived back in the northeast. We hated the distance between us. One of the family techniques to deal with the separation was called a "halfway trip," in which Christopher and I would meet my mother, my sister and my brother-in-law in Ohio, or essentially, half the distance for a weekend at a bed & breakfast. It worked beautifully and we had great fun visiting small towns in the Midwest while we kept our relationships close.

The trip in March of 2000 took place in a small, beautiful town in New Hampshire. There was still plenty of snow on the ground and we went hiking and on a tour of a local maple syrup farm.

After the husbands went to bed, my mother, sister and I sat up, talking into the wee hours of the morning. My mother still grieved enormously, as we all did, over the loss of my father, but the frequent visits helped to fill the enormous hole left by his death.

The clock on the bedside table said 1 a.m. and the conversation switched from funny to serious.

"I'm concerned," said my mother.

"I am too," chimed my sister.

"Concerned about what?" I asked.

"I want to know," my mother replied, now with passion, "Where did she go? Where did our girl go? Your life seems to be all about Christopher's life. Your career is second to his. Where you live is dictated by his job, but most of all, I wonder where our girl went – the one who had all the dreams of adventure and living a unique, extraordinary life? Is this really what you want?"

I thought for a long minute. I wasn't sure. But I knew she was right. Somehow, the love between Christopher and me had died, a slow and quiet death grown out of neglect. Our entire life seemed to be about his success. Somewhere along the way my fiery spirit had become quieter as I filled the role of his wife.

My mother was voicing something that I knew already.

"How did you know it was time to leave your first husband?" I asked a friend in late May.

She was my mother's age and associated with the University of Michigan, where I was working at night on my MBA. She had become a friend and mentor. I looked at her now over a cup of coffee at the diner near her house and wondered what her answer would be.

"I'll tell you something about my first marriage. When I realized that the relationship was not what I wanted and that our love had ended, I thought about what to do. And then I woke up one morning and said 'Today is the day.' And that was it."

Her story turned out to be similar to my own.

Three months later, in August, I woke up and thought, "Today is the day."

Christopher moved out three weeks later.

I pulled into the drive at the house in Michigan – the house that Christopher and I had shared. He had removed the last of his things and in doing so left me little notes on index cards – how to start the lawnmower, how to reset the fuse box.

I sat on the couch.

What to do first?

I had no idea.

The next day I stood in front of the fish case at the grocery store and pondered what to buy. There was no Christopher. It was *my* choice now.

And with the confusion came my old friend.

Up in the morning.
I'll just have a glass of milk.
The less, the better.
Have to stay thin.
Have to stay thin.
Have to be thin or no one will want me.
Ravenously hungry by lunch.
Burger, fries, lots of milk or ice cream (The ice cream made it easier to get rid of the food).
So hungry.
Down the food so fast that I hardly taste it.
Filling my stomach takes the emptiness away.
But now ...
Familiar panic ... I feel too full ... I'll get fat ... have to get rid of it.
Have to be thin.
Have to stay in control.
In the bathroom, first two fingers down my throat.
All the food comes up in a soupy mixture, down the toilet.
Clean up my face and my hands, leave the bathroom with a smile.
No one is the wiser.
2 p.m. Starving – my blood sugar is low, my body is so confused by the fact that there was food ... now there's none.
My hands shake from hunger.

Now I'll eat anything I can get my hands on.
Try to fill the emptiness.
Find an excuse to leave the office, binge on ice cream or cake.
Back to the office, back to the bathroom.
Purge again.
Same at 5:00 pm.
Home at 6:00.
Maybe binge and purge one more time.
Cookies from the convenience store or doughnuts from the shop down the street.
Eat them all in a flash, then throw them up.
Two or three vodka tonics.
In bed by 7:30.
My bedroom is dark and I'm under the covers.
Here I'm safe.
My body aches.
I just have to take the next breath.
I just have to take ... the next breath.

125 pounds.

I am the skinniest I've ever been.

My hipbone is close to the surface and I love the way it feels.

If nothing else, I am thin.

24

2001
No matter where I go, no matter what I do, I'm thinking about "the fix."

Where will I get food to binge?

Where is the bathroom where I can purge?

I am now an addict in every sense of the word.

Binging and purging four to five times per day. Every day.

My life is unrecognizable.

It is … no life.

Under the covers at night, I wish for the world to disappear.

Maybe tomorrow will magically be different. Maybe I'll stop the cycle.

But I can't.

Instead I get up to weigh myself for the tenth time that day.

And to find cookies or ice cream to satisfy my craving to binge.

In less than 25 minutes it will be down the toilet.

And this went on … for *eighteen months.*

25

April 2002.

My mother and my sister, Beth, pulled into the driveway. They were visiting to celebrate my graduation from the MBA program at the University of Michigan Business School.

I came out to the porch to welcome them.

I was thin.

124 pounds.

On my medium frame the lower weight looked boney ... gaunt. My eyes were exhausted and watery. My skin was pale and pasty. My salivary glands were inflamed from constant vomiting and my face had a "square" look, with swelling in the lower part of my cheeks.

My mother stepped from the car. She looked across the hood to my sister.

"She looks terrible."

The next morning my sister cornered me in the bathroom.

"You don't look like yourself. You look ... unhappy," Beth said to me, "It seems like something's wrong. What is it?"

I felt trapped. At the same time I recognized the hell that my life had become. For nearly two years I had binged and purged four to five times per day. I didn't remember anymore what it felt like to be normal. I knew I needed help. But I was so ... ashamed. So overwhelmed with self-disgust.

"Whatever this is, whatever you're going through, you *know* you can tell us," my sister continued.

"I don't know if I can tell you *this*," I said.

Beth put her hands on my arms.

"Tell me."

"I love you Beth. And I trust you," I whispered.

But I still hesitated.

"What is it?" she pressed.

"I'm sick Beth, and I don't know how to get well. I don't ... I don't know how to fix this."

I was weeping now, my shoulders shaking with emotion.

"I'm bulimic," I whispered.

"Okay?" she replied, "What does that mean?"

"I eat sometimes and then I feel desperate and afraid that I'll gain weight, so I make myself throw up," I replied.

"Why?" she asked in amazement and surprise.

"I have to be thin. I'll do *anything* to be thin. I'm a size 4 now and I want to stay that size. But I get so hungry and then I end up eating everything in sight. Then I feel panic, like I have to get rid of it."

"Okay," she said again, "how often does this happen?"

I closed my eyes and hung my head in misery and shame.

"A few times per day," I replied.

It was later that Beth told me of her conversation with my mother in the days that followed.

"What do you mean she gets *sick*," my mother asked my sister incredulously, "On *purpose?* How can this be happening? She's such an intelligent girl!"

"I don't understand it either Mom," my sister replied, "but I don't think it has to do with intelligence. I think it's more like alcoholism or some sort of addiction. This is serious – she needs professional help."

"Like what?" my mother asked.

"Like *professional* help ... a doctor for sure, maybe a psychiatrist. We have to help her. Her life is out of control and I'm not sure she can help herself. There's a psychological component, like she doesn't know how to stop doing it. The way she said it – she'll do *anything* to be thin – like she's obsessed."

There was a long silence.

"Do you think we need to hospitalize her?" my mother asked, still in disbelief.

My sister pondered the question, "Let's see if we can get her to come home."

26

August 2002.

"Are you *better?*" my mother asked firmly.

Her "no nonsense" voice.

Five minutes before dialing she had decided that her patience was at an end.

"*Are* you better?" she asked again.

Silence.

"Better how?" I quipped.

"Don't give me lip, you know what I mean. Is it still happening? Are you still destroying yourself and your life? Are you still throwing up?"

"Yes," I replied quietly.

"How many times?"

"Four."

"This week?"

"Today."

"That's *it* Jenifer. You're *done*. You've tried it on your own and it isn't working. Now you come home and get well."

"Uh huh," I replied with reluctance.

"Jenifer, I mean business," my mother responded.

The conversation ended there but I grasped the unspoken meaning. I either came home of my own volition or they would arrive unannounced to take me by force.

My family had no intention of letting me throw my life away.

After their visit to see me in Michigan and learning of my bulimia, Beth and my mother had mobilized. Beth researched bulimia nervosa and learned about treatment options. She had attended a girls' college in Philadelphia and during her

time there came to know of the Renfrew Center, a treatment
facility for women with eating disorders. In her research she
discovered that there was another facility in Connecticut, near
our family cottage where my mother lived. Meanwhile, my
mother began preparations for me to move home. The tiny
guestroom with its antique bed was made up with fresh
sheets, ready for my arrival.

October 2002.

"It's time to get up," my mother said cheerfully.

I opened my eyes reluctantly.

Her voice was kind but firm. She pulled the covers back
and reached for my feet. Pulling them over the side of the
bed, she sat me up.

"The first step is to put your feet on the floor," she continued, "We have to go, so let's get dressed."

She opened the shades.

"It's time for you to take your life *back*."

It was time to begin treatment at the Renfrew Center[41] in
Wilton, Connecticut.

My mother drove me there to make sure that there were
no detours for doughnuts.

129 pounds.

On the first day of treatment I was more interested in the
fact that my weight was up four pounds than in the fact that I
was about to start treatment for my eating disorder.

I thought about that number all day.

129.

---

[41] The Renfrew Center began in 1985 with one facility in Philadelphia
focused on treating women with eating disorders. Today the network includes eight treatment centers and a worldwide network of health care
professionals and nutritionists. With both residential and outpatient
treatment programs, Renfrew focuses on behavioral change and treating
the underlying issues that cause a woman to become anorexic or bulimic.
Their innovative approach incorporates personalized treatment tailored
for each woman's individual needs. The program insists on the personal
commitment and involvement of the patient as a part of recovery.

Ronia's office looked more like a boudoir than the professional setting of a Harvard trained psychologist. There were funny chaise-like chairs, a multi-colored circa 1970's carpet, mobiles and something that looked suspiciously like a bong. Ronia is Israeli, straight off the boat.

She looked at me over her notepad.

"Are you ready to get well?" Ronia asked.

Her voice was gentle but I sensed strength and seriousness.

"I want to get well, but I don't want to be fat. I'll die first," I replied.

"If you don't get well, you might get your wish," said Ronia slowly.

She paused to let me digest her words.

"We are going to try outpatient therapy first. We'll try that for a few weeks but if you aren't making progress I suggest you become a resident here. You won't get fat under our care," she continued, "We want you to be at a healthy weight but in a *healthy* way."

I nodded ... gratefully ... and reluctantly.

Ronia looked at me thoughtfully.

"Let's get started. Tell me the lowest point. What was the moment you knew that you did not control your bulimia. That it controlled you?"

"You mean in terms of negative behavior?"

"What is this 'negative behavior' bullshit? Say the word!" said Ronia, "Say the word 'bulimia!' Call it by name. When you can call it by name and own it, you take away its power."

"Okay ... the lowest point of the ... bulimia ... "

I thought for a moment.

"There was one night. I had been shopping and I was driving home. I was suddenly *starving* ... so hungry ...I couldn't even wait to get to the house. I stopped at a convenience store and bought every cookie and chip I could get my hands on. I started binging on the food in the convenience store, stuffing the chips into my mouth. I kept eating in the car while I drove. I ate every morsel and was completely stuffed. But as I drove back home there were no gas stations or rest stops with a bathroom and I *had* to get rid of the food ... I was ... *desperate.*"

"Then what happened?" she probed.

The office was quiet.

"I'm so ... *ashamed*," I said, looking at the floor.

Ronia leaned forward in her chair.

"I know, but you can do it ... put it into words," she responded gently, "When you say the words you own the problem. When you own the problem, you get to own the solution."

I nodded.

The words stuck as they came out.

"It was dark. I figured that no one would see me. So I pulled over to the side of the road, got out and made myself sick right there on the highway with the cars going by. I figured they didn't know who I was, I'd never see them again, so why should I care if they saw me?"

Ronia nodded.

"Tell me another story."

"One time I was traveling for business. There had been a big breakfast meeting and I had eaten way too much. I was so desperate to purge that I ended up in the restroom at this disgusting gas station on the side of the road. There were puddles of urine on the floor. When I threw up, part of the vomit went into the puddles and the urine splattered. The water faucet didn't work so I couldn't wash my face or my hands. So there I was, splattered with someone else's pee, vomit on my mouth and hands. I did my best to clean up and then got back in the car and drove to my next meeting."

"Addiction has no pride," Ronia said.

"*No* pride," I echoed, nodding, "There were times I would have done anything to satisfy my desire to binge and purge. Told any lie. Plus I never wanted my job to be affected."

"So you're a functioning bulimic," Ronia responded.

"My professional life has never missed a beat."

Ronia nodded. She had seen hundreds of anorexics and bulimics. She knew every scenario, every line, every cover story. She was tougher than dirt and determined to help her patients get well.

"So when we're sick, we work to get *well*. Let's write about that this week. Write about your friend, your bulimia. This is your homework"

Then Ronia wrote down the names of the rest of my treatment team – a psychiatrist who would assess my need for prescription medication and a dietician who would help me learn to eat again.

The next day my mother and I sat across from the psychiatrist in his opulent office. There were beautiful suede couches in an unusual color and the carpet on the floor was Turkish. He even had a beautiful pen.

"I guess this is what happens when you charge $400 per hour," I whispered to my mother. She just nodded. She was busy examining the piece of baccarat crystal on the end table.

Dr. Reynolds began scribbling, asking questions about my mood, sleeping habits and alcohol intake. He curved his left hand over the paper so he could write.

"So what happens in the morning when you get up?" he asked.

"I don't really want to get up, but when I do, I start out wanting to have a 'good day' ..."

"What's a good day?" Dr. Reynolds asked.

"One with no bulimia," I replied.

"Is that realistic?" he asked.

"I always want it to be," I replied, "but then by late morning I am craving food, craving the fix."

"What do you binge on?"

"Snack food mostly," I said, "Cookies, chips, ice cream."

"At ten in the morning?"

"Uh huh."

"Then what do you feel?" he asked.

"Panic," I replied.

"Panic that you'll gain weight."

"Yes ... it's like terror."

He scribbled some more.

"Do you think about suicide?" he asked, switching topics abruptly.

I could see my mother visibly cringe in the chair and at that moment I was filled with regret as I realized what my addiction must be doing to her.

"No," I replied truthfully, "I sometimes hate being alive and the pain of it, but I haven't ever considered ending my life."

"Fair enough," he replied.

The hour wound on.

"Are you caring for yourself in other ways?" he asked.

I shot him a look of confusion.

"Did you brush your teeth today?" he asked.

I shook my head. There were tears there, just behind my eyes.

"I'm not trying to embarrass you Jenifer. But I have to assess where you are right now."

I nodded miserably.

"So you haven't brushed your teeth lately?"

"A couple of weeks ago maybe ... it's all I can do just to ... exist," I replied softly.

"So you're in a state of self neglect," he said with kindness.

The room was quiet.

"When things seem particularly sad to you, how do you cope other than with your bulimia?" he continued.

"I love to be in bed at night. I close the shades and it's warm under the covers. I feel safe. Sometimes I hurt so much that my body aches. At moments like that I tell myself, 'You just have to take the next breath.' ... Just the next breath."

He nodded. There was compassion on his face.

"Well, it's obvious that you're clinically depressed. What often happens with eating disorders is that the bulimia and the depression feed each other. The more you purge, the more ashamed you are and the more depressed you become.

The more depressed you become, the more you want to binge, which of course leads immediately to purging, and so on. It becomes its own endless cycle. So let's see if we can get the depression under control during the next few weeks. I think that will help you with your treatment program as well."

"I've been on antidepressants before," I replied with skepticism, "while I lived in Michigan. I kept thinking they would make the bulimia better, but they didn't."

"That's because you need the rest of the treatment program along with the medication. The prescription isn't an instant fix."

"There's no magic solution, is there?" I said slowly.

"No Jenifer, there's not," he replied, "But you *can* get well. It's just going to take a lot of work."

And he wrote out the prescription.

The following day I met with Ann Marie, the dietician. Her office was professional, but more cheerful than stern, with a Snoopy motif everywhere. The first step was to be weighed and I felt myself becoming uneasy.

She must have seen it on my face.

"Don't worry, the weighing is just for me, so that we can keep on eye on what your body is doing while you're in treatment. How often do you weigh at home?"

"Ten, maybe twelve times per day," I replied.

She nodded, "Well, that's going to stop now. The healthiest choice is to weigh once per week, but we realize that this may not be possible with your eating disorder, so we're just going to try and get it down to once a day, okay? You weigh once in the morning with all your clothes off, and then that's it. Put the scale away where it's harder to access. Don't just leave it out on the floor in the bathroom."

She took out a clipboard with a bunch of forms and little pictures of fruits and vegetables.

"Okay, step up on the scale backwards. From now on, whenever you weigh, whether it's in a doctors office or whatever, if it isn't your scale that you weigh on, you weigh backwards and ask them not to tell you the number. That number becomes a huge source of stress and we have to remove that."

Dutifully, I turned around with my back to the sliding rod on the scale. Ann Marie moved it along until it balanced and wrote the number down, all out of my sight.

My mind went back to being "taped" on the West Point Weight Program. This measuring process was completely different.

It was caring. Supportive.

Ann Marie went over a detailed food plan with a certain number of proteins, carbohydrates, milk, etc. I would prepare and measure all of my own food.

"This is important," she said, "Because as you prepare your own food, you invest in your health. And you learn good eating habits that will nourish and strengthen your body. Oatmeal is your friend. It's only 160 calories for a cup of cooked oatmeal, very filling, warm, comforting, and the carbohydrates will tide you over til the next meal. Every meal is small and two hours apart. The trick for a bulimic is to eat small amounts every two hours on the dot. By doing that, you'll never feel so full that you'll want to purge and you'll never be so hungry that you'll want to binge. It won't work perfectly in the beginning, but when you want to binge, try eating your oatmeal and wait twenty minutes. If you still want to binge, fine, but as you progress in your treatment that will often be enough to keep you from running to the candy or chips."

I nodded as she spoke.

"There are rules too," she continued, "make sure you have a snack at least 20 minutes before you go to the grocery store. And for now, no eating out."

So with my little food guide in tow, off I went.

"We have to stop at the food store," I said to my mother as I got in the car.

"What are we getting?" she asked.

"Oatmeal."

128 pounds.

27

Ronia looked at me from across her pad of paper. I was two weeks into the program and saw her every few days. The sessions were difficult. I felt like I was digging things out of the open sores in my life.

"Tell me about your husband," she said.

Sadness came over me like a blanket.

"We were so in love at first ... I didn't think I could breathe if he wasn't in my life," I said, "But there were conditions. I think I knew instinctively that things could never be too difficult for him or he would leave. And then he did. When he didn't fight to save our marriage I felt so unwanted and rejected."

"There's a theme here," she said, "men and their approval. You fought for your father's approval, then your classmates at West Point, then your squad leader, then your husband."

I nodded, "If they didn't approve of me, I wasn't good enough."

"Good enough for what?" Ronia asked thoughtfully.

"I'm not even sure," I said wryly.

"Let's write about that this week," said Ronia.

There was always homework.

A lot of homework.

A lot of work, period.

I discovered that getting well was the hardest thing I had ever done.

Harder than jumping out of an airplane.

Harder than West Point.

I saw the members of my treatment team regularly. I shopped for and prepared my own food. There was no eating out at restaurants. I took my medication faithfully each morning. And I was never alone. I was with a family member from the moment I woke up in the morning until the moment my head hit the pillow at night. If my mother went to church choir practice, I went to church choir practice. When my sister went shopping, she called me to come along, picked me up and took me with her, and then dropped me off at my mother's when we were finished. When there was a formal anniversary dinner for a friend of my mother's, she called ahead and communicated that she would be bringing her daughter, invited or not. She and my sister checked in with Ronia by phone.

They were all relentless.

This was war.

The preparation of my food became my daily routine, caring for myself enough to shop for healthy fruits and vegetables to make into snacks and meals each day. I ate "safe" food – unsweetened oatmeal, soft cooked eggs, granola bars. I ate every two hours on the nose and crossed off the little food plan checkboxes with each meal or snack.

The first three weeks were the hardest. I craved the fix.

"Try to extend the time between your binging," Ronia said, "If you want to binge at 2:00, try to put it off til three."

My schedule became methodical and reminiscent of military challenges at West Point like the infamous IOCT where I attacked the challenge one small part at a time. The daily schedule became the shelf.

7 a.m. Out of bed.
Run up to the shelf.
8 a.m. 1 cup cooked oatmeal.
Jump up, grab the edge.
10 a.m. Granola bar.
Pull up.
Noon. 1 cup cooked pasta, tiny bit of olive oil, tomatoes and 3 oz. chicken

Stomach muscles.
2 p.m. Piece of fruit.
Make myself into a little ball.
4 p.m. 1 cup cooked oatmeal or granola bar and hot tea.
Hook the foot, pull up, shelf into the crotch.
6 p.m. Dinner with the family – a starch, vegetables, 3-4 oz. protein.
*Right thigh folded on top, push, push, **push...***
8 p.m. Snack, usually fruit, hot herbal tea.
Torso on top...
10 p.m. Bed.
Victory.

With "the schedule," therapy, my daily medication and meetings with the dietician, I achieved small victories – a morning without binging and purging, or an afternoon. I saw the possibility of getting well. I cooked every morsel of food that I ate, investing in my own health by choosing my groceries and preparing the food that nourished my body. With each batch of oatmeal I made, I took a step toward getting well.

I began to remember what it felt like to feel legitimately hungry.

And what it felt like to be comfortably full.

I began to believe that I deserved better than an eating disorder.

By the end of the fourth week, I had my first healthy day -- bulimia free -- in eighteen months.

On a morning during the fourth week I got up out of bed without my mother's help. Naked, I went out to the bathroom and pulled out the scale and stepped on it.

128 pounds.

True to Ronia's promise, I hadn't gained an ounce since starting treatment.

As I stood there on the scale and began to step off, my mother appeared from her bedroom.

She was weeping.

She took me in her arms even as I was standing on the scale.

"You *have* to get well, you just have to get well," she wept, "I can't lose you."

I started to cry.

My eating disorder didn't belong only to me.

"Mom, I'm workin' on it. I'm really trying," I whispered.

"I know, I know … just please get well. Please get well."

"I'm trying Mom," I said with a sob.

We stood there for ten minutes, just holding each other.

"Addiction is hard on families," Ronia said the next day.

"I feel so guilty for what I've done to them," I replied.

"We can't focus on that though, we have to focus on the positive," she replied, "Your family loves you and they are treating this just as if you had a physical ailment versus an addiction. You would do the same for them, right?"

I nodded, "Of course."

"Our culture is built around being thin," Ronia continued, "so much so that even when we are making ourselves throw up, the world applauds the thinness of our body, reinforcing the bulimia. There's a drive in our culture for women to be perfect, physically and otherwise, and this feeds the bulimia as well."

"When I went to the ten year reunion of my West Point class in 2001, I was bulimic every day," I replied, "The pattern of binging and purging had taken over my life. But everyone at the reunion said, 'You look great' and it was validation after those years of criticism."

"That validation becomes its own form of addiction," Ronia commented.

I nodded.

"I told them I was eating right and exercising. What a joke. Meanwhile, I threw up twice during the reunion dinner."

"So what have you learned?" asked Ronia.

"That I have to validate myself. That my own voice and the right to be healthy has to be stronger than the validation of others."

Ronia nodded ... and gave me more homework.

During treatment, some days were good, some not so good.

At a neighborhood picnic one piece of pie turned into six pieces of pie and my head in our neighbor's toilet.

"Why aren't you asking for help? You need to find your voice," Ronia said. "Your family loves you. Tell them what you need. When you are in danger, ask for help."

At a dinner party the following week, I eyed the home-made macaroni and cheese on the table. I had already eaten one serving. I heard the familiar voice telling me that I had to stop or be forced to get rid of the food.

"Can you take that away?" I asked my sister.

Without batting an eye, my sister moved the casserole dish. She had been to her session with Ronia. Under the table she took my hand and squeezed it.

About the sixth week of treatment, I sat down with my checkbook and added up what I was paying to treat my addiction.

The amount was staggering.

My mother came into the room, curious to see what I was doing. This was a time in my life where I had little privacy and kept few secrets. She and my sister were fully enmeshed in my every day and it seemed pointless to hide things.

"What is this costing you?" my mother asked, taking in the checkbook register.

"You can't believe it," I replied in disbelief, "Thousands ..."

I was lucky. I had it to spend. As a part of our divorce, Christopher and I had sold our house in Michigan in the days of the housing boom and I had made some money. It was now paying for my treatment.

"What do people do who can't afford this?" my mother said, looking over my shoulder.

"I don't know Mom," I replied with a shake of my head.

The following week, Ronia made a list of doctors for me to see. The physical toll that an eating disorder takes on the body is significant and as the focus of the program was on becoming entirely healthy, Ronia sent me to one physician after another.

The first examined my throat and esophagus to assess the damage after nearly thirteen years of abuse. By some miracle, everything appeared to be fine. The same doctor talked with me about eating enough fiber, as my system seemed to be entirely screwed up and irregular. The oatmeal was helping but we added dried fruit.

Next stop was the dermatologist. Months of dehydration had aggravated my skin and my back was full of acne.

Finally, the dentist.

Dr. Salvo looked down at me with a smile and moved the light so that he could examine my gums. I reached up and stopped his hand. Ronia's words echoed in my head.

Find your voice.

"I'm in treatment."

I shook as I said the words.

Call it by name.

"I'm in treatment for … bulimia," I continued.

"How long have you been sick?" he asked.

He was concerned.

"Thirteen years," I replied.

He put his hand on my shoulder.

"And how long have you been in recovery?"

"Forty four days, six hours," I choked.

He looked into my face with compassion.

"That's an accomplishment!" he replied, "Now let's take a look."

He moved the light again and looked into my mouth, pricking my teeth with a metal pick.

"Well, I thought it might be worse," he said through his mask, "Bulimics often strip all the enamel off their teeth. You got lucky I think. How often were you purging?"

"During the last year and a half it was three to five times per day," I replied.

It was easier to answer the questions now. Dr. Salvo wasn't judging me. He didn't exhibit disgust at the thought of my intentional vomiting.

He was compassionate.

"Wow," he shook his head in disbelief, "but it sounds like you're well into treatment. The key is to keep working at it. I imagine you know that by now."

I nodded.

"You'll beat it," he smiled and, patting me on the shoulder, got up to write on my chart.

Over eight long months, I slowly recovered. I faithfully prepared my food each day, placing it in neatly stacked plastic containers in the fridge. I did the homework that Ronia assigned, mostly writing exercises in which I explored the losses in my life and my need to please other people. I followed every step and obeyed every edict. Every so often I would become overwhelmed and would find a toilet to get rid of a snack or a meal, but the intervals in between became longer and longer.

First weeks.

Then months.

Slowly, my life returned.

129 pounds.

But healthy.

28

You need to get a job," my mother said over a biteful of zucchini.

"Yup," my sister agreed, nodding her head.

We were having dinner at my mother's house.

February 2003.

"I am working," I replied hastily.

"You're working part-time and your job has served its purpose, we all know this is not where you need to be in your professional life. It's time to put that MBA to use."

"I'm still … unsure," I said quietly. I was pushing the rice around my plate, listening to my inner voice. I had had enough. I was full. I handed the plate to my sister, who promptly took it away.

"I think it's time for a new experience, the next step in your life outside of the treatment program," said my mother.

"Have you been talking to Ronia?" I replied with a smile.

"I think it's time for you to be in our wonderful city. It's time for a little adventure," my mother said with a definitive nod.

The Henry Hudson turned into the West Side Highway as I drove into New York. The clock on the dash said 2:00 and my interview was at 4:00. It had snowed the night before, leaving New York City white and beautiful. I turned onto 50th Street and watched as people trudged by in their snow boots. Ten minutes passed, then twenty and I was still on the west side. Cross-town traffic was at a standstill. The interview was on the east side and I was ten blocks away.

"I'll have to hoof it," I thought.

Pulling into the next garage, I grabbed my briefcase and, wrapping my coat around me, started on foot for the other side of the city.

It felt great to be out in the fresh air. The strength of my body and mind was returning. With my depression and bulimia under control and my health improving, everything seemed full of possibility.

I was deep in thought as I started across Fifth Avenue.

Things were taking a turn for the better. I could sense it.

And then ...

Sploosh!

I stepped off the curb ... and was calf high in cold, wet, snowy slush.

I scrambled out of the ice water and looked down in horror at my pantsuit, which was now soaked to the knee. I had been so lost in thought that I had forgotten to step over the "lake" at the edge of the avenue.

"How could I forget my boots?" I chided myself.

Determined to make the best of it, I ploughed ahead. But the water at the sides of each avenue only got wider, until my pants were soaked to mid thigh and my high heels squelched with every step.

As I crossed Lexington and waded across yet another pool of slush, the hilarity of the situation took hold. With my brisk pace I would likely make the interview on time, but with my suit wet up to my crotch.

I started to laugh.

The briskness of my walk was keeping me warm. The icy water in which I waded was uncomfortable, but not a real threat. As my father said so many times, "What's the worst that could happen?"

What's the worst that could happen?

I looked at my sodden shoes and continued to laugh.

And then, standing on the corner of Lexington and 50th, I started to cry.

I realized the truth -- the worst that could happen at this moment in my life was to be sick again. The wet slacks and ruined high heels didn't matter at all.

The only thing that mattered was a life without the prison of addiction.

I was well -- and thankful.

October 2004.

It had been a full year since the start of treatment. It had been nearly six months since I had purged. I had taken a great new job with a marketing firm and I was well enough to travel and eat at restaurants.

"What do you feel now?" asked Ronia, "What do you feel now that you are sober?"

"I'm on the end of the diving board, ready to leap off into a marvelous adventure" I smiled, "I feel like everything is ahead."

Ronia nodded, "What else?"

"Relief I think, just grateful to have my life back, to have broken the cycle of the bulimia, to be healthy ... so grateful to my family ... and to you." I replied with affection.

"These are all good, healthy thoughts," Ronia said, " but now you must work hard and must be committed every day to making positive choices, to staying well, to staying healthy. You will *always* be bulimic. You must never forget that. So you must always be on your guard. But if you use the tools you've learned here, you can live the marvelous life that you are meant to live. And your mother, your sister and I will be here when you need us."

The office was quiet. But she wasn't finished.

"There is more to all of this I think. We've talked about the people who were so influential in your life, mostly men – your father, your husband, men in your career. When you said good-bye to your bulimia you said good-bye to the need to please other people."

She was right.

They were all gone. Every last one of them had disappeared.

"What is it that you *really* feel Jenny?" Ronia whispered, leaning forward. "What do you feel now that you define yourself, now that your bulimia no longer runs your life. What do you really feel?"

"*Free,*" I whispered back, "I *finally* feel free."

29

November 2004.
The bar at the Watergate Hotel.

I had flown to Washington D.C. to attend Tennessee Williams' *Cat on a Hot Tin Roof*, which was playing at the Kennedy Center. I was doing the unthinkable – going to the theater without a date. I was learning how to be happy as a single person, stepping out into new adventures of travels and activities, sometimes alone, sometimes with friends or family. My bulimia was at bay and it seemed like the world stretched in front of me like an amazing adventure.

He walked over casually, adjusting the bill of his baseball cap like a woman tosses her hair. He was tan and shot me a sly smile of capped white teeth.

"I never do this," he said.

Uh huh.

I could smell the gin on his breath. The conversation was primarily one-sided and I was eager to end it so I simply handed him my business card and said, "Tell ya what, here's my card and if you wake up in the morning and you reeeallly want to talk to me, here's how to reach me."

And then I turned, left him standing there and assumed in his liquor-soaked state he would remember none of the exchange.

The next day he called. Turned out he was a writer.

About two months into the relationship I met with Ronia for one of our sessions. We continued to meet regularly as I worked at staying well. I didn't feel the daily urge to binge and purge but I still had to be cautious, using the tools I had learned during treatment.

Ronia looked at me from across the room. She was the same level-headed guide she had been from the start. She also had some new rules now that I was officially in recovery. Any new relationship was to be discussed during our sessions and, if someone was a candidate to be a long-term partner, he would have to meet with her. In Ronia's world, there was no kissing away sobriety just because a handsome face came along.

"So he's been calling," I told her about "Tanqueray."

"You really like this man," she said, "Have you said anything to him?"

"I'm afraid to tell him," I said to her.

"Tell him . . . " Ronia prompted.

"I'm afraid to tell him that I'm bulimic," I said dutifully.

"You don't have to wear a sign that says you have an eating disorder, but if you were ever to be with someone long-term, you would need to share this truth about yourself. And if that person, whoever he is, doesn't understand or have compassion for what you've fought to overcome, then that person cannot be in your life. It's that simple. You understand that, right?"

I nodded. This is one of the rules of being in recovery.

A few weeks later I sat with Tanqueray in his living room. There were candles lit, Gershwin playing. It was romantic. It didn't feel like a great moment to introduce my history with, "Oh, by the way, just wanted to mention that I occasionally make myself throw up, and also, that after thirteen years of bulimia I had to move into my mother's house in 2002 in order to go through treatment and get well."

But as Ronia pointed out, this wasn't going to get easier with time. So I took a big breath and walked him through it.

To his credit, he listened. He sympathized. But the connection he couldn't make was how the binge-purge cycle can become addictive. Food is necessary for human life. It was incomprehensible to him that the emotion and dysfunction that surround an eating disorder can become much like any other addiction. For a bulimic, the urge to binge and purge can take over to the point that some bulimics will do anything a drug addict would do in order to satisfy the craving.

Really … *anything.*

Addiction knows no pride.

He didn't get it.

A week later we went to see Swan Lake at the Kennedy Center. The ballet was spectacular and afterwards we went out for Thai food.

"I think you should write something," he said to me over a spring roll.

I had always scribbled in journals, but mostly ramblings fueled by my thoughts and experiences. I had never been serious about writing a book.

"Have that last spring roll," he said to me, pushing it my way with a chopstick.

"No," I replied, listening to my body, "I've had enough."

"Then it's just going to go to waste," he replied with criticism.

"No … thank you," I replied firmly.

He just didn't get it.

Not long after we parted ways.

To this day I can't stand the smell of Tanqueray.

But I gained one thing from the relationship with him … the decision to write a book … a book about my eating disorder and my journey to get well.

In early 2005 I began to write every morning. I rose at 5:20 a.m. like those days so long ago when we awoke at West Point to the sound of MacArthur's speech blasted through the barracks. Bleary-eyed, I would take my coffee and sit at my desk with a blanket over my legs, typing away on my computer.

By late in 2006, the first draft of the book was finished. The story of my experience at West Point and my bulimia were told in the third person and the book was entitled, "The Freedom of Jane Renault." Jane was our young heroine who goes off to West Point and has a series of Private Benjamin-like adventures, only to succumb to pressure from all side to lose weight. She becomes bulimic and must find her life and her freedom again through treatment and the support of her family.

When I was finished, I printed it out and it sat on my lap in a big stack of paper.

And I had no idea what to do with it.

I knew nothing about the business of publishing a book. But I did know plenty about business and one thing I had learned in my first marketing job was that the number one way to learn about something new is to network with those who are in the know.

And that is how I found Liz.

It was a cold day in January when I drove into New York to meet Liz Fitzgerald, an editor who came highly recommended by a friend of my mother.

"I don't know if she'll take you on as a client," the acquaintance said to me over the phone, "but why don't you see if she'll meet with you."

Liz was and is a true New Yorker. She's lived for twenty years in the City, on the Lower, lower, loooowwweer East Side and remembers the day when there was gunfire in the streets. She worked for a publisher for a number of years and now does editing for select writers who are serious about their work.

And the key word is *serious*.

I left my car at a garage in midtown and cabbed it down to a part of the city that was new to me. The buildings whizzed by. And with each passing block there was more of the neighborhood feel that still exists on the Lower East Side. Small shops passed and small restaurants, the kind that have just five tables and lots of personality.

Liz and I met in the back room of a tiny coffee shop. There was hideous orange carpet on the floor and an old sofa. I shook her hand and noticed her smile. Liz is a woman who knows who she is. In the space of thirty seconds I recognized that Liz would be a great ally. I sensed that she would tell me the truth.

And it was as crystal clear as the day is long -- I was being interviewed.

"I wanted to see what you'd look like on TV," she said after we'd talked for a bit.

Then she said the words I'll never forget.

"It's a good story," she said, "but I think you have to decide whether or not you want to really tell this story and own it. As the reader we kind of get that you're Jane but we don't really know for sure. This story would be enormously more compelling if you would tell it in the first person. But you have to decide whether you are ready to do that. If you are, then I'll work with you on it."

The naked truth of course was that it felt so much safer to hide behind the character of Jane Renault. Then I wouldn't have to actually *say the word*. I wouldn't actually have to publicly own it.

Bulimia.

Say the word.

Even post treatment, as I lived a challenging and exciting professional life, traveling the world, living an amazing adventure, I still didn't want to say the words.

I am bulimic.

I drove back to Connecticut, thinking about Liz and our conversation, wondering if I had what it took to rewrite the entire book and to essentially "out" myself. No one at my workplace had any idea of my history. Hardly anyone knew my truth. Was I really ready to rip off the bandaid and expose it to all those who might laugh or sneer or criticize. What would my West Point classmates think? What would it mean for my life?

I slept on it for three weeks. And then one morning I woke up thinking of the Edmund Burke quote that has inspired me for years.

"All that is necessary for evil to triumph is for good men to do nothing."

So I could do ... nothing ... and not tell my story, and not feel that nerve-wracking feeling of stepping out on the edge when I tell people my truth and wonder if they'll judge me. I could walk away from this bulimia and all that it had been and is to this day in my life, keeping it my quiet secret.

Or I could have courage. I could be brave, and pray that the words of the book would be a blessing in some way to a woman who suffers from an eating disorder, or the family who are at their wit's end trying to figure out how to help her. I could write with the conviction that the story matters because nearly every woman I know thinks of her weight every day.

So I began the rewrite ...

30

... which took two years.

As I worked on recrafting the story in the first person, Liz worked with me while I developed the pace and rhythm of my style. I carefully constructed the words and phrases that told my story with all of its terrible darkness and all of its sense of hope. Writing about the worst time of my life was painful – painful when I had written it about the anonymous Jane Renault – more painful when I could not hide behind her character.

With the writing finished I again went to meet with Liz in the bowels of the City. It had been a blustery, rainy day, which in New York means one thing – no available taxi cabs. So I did what any enterprising young writer would do – I hailed a rickshaw.

"It's thirty blocks," I said to the bicycler, hoping he would consent.

He grinned, nodded and zipped open the plastic cover to the compartment inside.

I pulled my tote in behind me and prayed that the bicycler was athletic and speedy.

Down the avenue the rickshaw sailed with the raindrops smacking the bicycler and the plastic cover. The city was wet with rain, the sidewalks covered with open umbrellas. My driver seemed undaunted, however, and before long we were on the Lower East Side. I got out at the appointed location and struggled to open my umbrella while tipping the diligent fellow with genuine appreciation for his effort. I was on time.

Liz had arrived moments before me and sat at a little table in Starbucks with the manuscript in front of her. It lay in a box with a rubber band around it holding each page I had written with her line edits and grammatical corrections. She handed me the box with a smile.

"You should be very proud," she said with a smile.

I had done it. I had written the book. My book. My story. My truth.

My truth, but a story that so many American women relate to.

Because every woman I know thinks about her weight every day.

I am hardly alone.

Recently I was sitting on an airplane, getting ready to take off from Frankfurt to New York. The woman sitting next to me wanted to chat. As we were talking I mentioned that I was writing a book. She was curious to know what it was about and I told her ambiguously that it had to do with the pressure American women put on themselves to be physically perfect.

"I've been doing some research on this subject," I said, "and I wonder if you'd be willing to answer a question for me."

She nodded in reply and so I continued.

"How often do you think about your weight?" I asked.

"Constantly," she replied without missing a beat, "Every single day."

And this is the answer I get from the vast majority of women to whom I pose the question.

So many of us think about our weight ... every day.

So how do we stop the madness? How do we stop beating ourselves up and beating our bodies into submission? How do we stop trading our health for what society deems as physical perfection? Where does it stop? How do *we* stop it?

Part of the issue is societal. No question – thin is in! And it's not just "healthy thin." Instead it's "bone thin." We see it in fashion, on the red carpet, in film and in magazines. The imagery is a constant barrage of stimuli that tells us that thinner is better, no matter what it takes. And the deluge of messaging starts early. Barbie dolls, whose physicality are representative of essentially no women, signal to young girls at an early age that a skinny woman is successful, beautiful and loved. And the fashion models seem to just get thinner ... and thinner. As a part of my job I recently attended a photo shoot where one of the models admitted to us that she *had a rib removed* in order to be skinnier.

Many of us are willing to do ... anything.

Anything to be thin. Any price. Whatever the cost.

So the message of these pages is meant for every woman who wistfully looks at her "skinny jeans" sitting up on the closet shelf, for every anorexic or bulimic struggling to get well, for every young girl who thinks her adult body should be comparable to that of a Barbie doll, for every family who are desperate to help the woman they love who suffers from an eating disorder. And the message is this – anorexia and bulimia are everywhere – on every campus, in every community, among college students, adolescent girls, housewives and professionals. And it is only with deliberate effort that things will change.

This year marks seven years since I completed the treatment program at the Renfrew Center in Wilton, Connecticut. It has been six months since my last purge, and eighteen months the time before that. But it is always there, the demon that claimed to be my friend.

I am in recovery but my bulimia will never disappear. It is simply being managed. And it must be managed every single day.

I will always be bulimic.

I will always be an addict.

But in recovery from addiction I have the freedom to live a magnificent life.

And if I can get well – you can too.

And where are the players now?

My ex-husband, who I still claim as a true love of my life, continued on with a successful career in law enforcement. He is married now and has a son. We connect every so often to say hello. He is, by all appearances, living a happy life, but a life different from the one I ultimately wanted and I am convinced our divorce was the right decision. I sometimes take out the love letters he wrote me, the little papers he sent from Ranger School or the notes he tucked under my windshield when we were new second lieutenants at Fort Hood. I keep them carefully packed away in a box and have never been able to bear the thought of throwing them away. I think of that crazy passion we had when we were just twenty-two and doubt I will ever love like that again. I feel lucky to have loved like that at all.

My classmates at West Point all traveled an assortment of paths. I see Jill, my Beast roommate, on Facebook. We recently corresponded via email and she is living a happy, fulfilled life. Katherine McNeil and I remained friends for years. Matt Bailey went on to be a successful entrepreneur and committed family man out west, and we exchange a note now and then.

West Point for me is inextricably entangled in the bulimia that nearly took my freedom and my life. It's hard for me to disconnect the two, and so I am satisfied to watch the comings and goings of the Academy from afar.

Do I blame the Academy or my dad or anyone else for my bulimia? Absolutely not. But my story is similar to other bulimics I've spoken to – it's not a single event or comment that pushes someone over the edge. It is the wearing down of the spirit one small bit at a time, like water wears a hole in a stone. One little comment followed by another disparaging remark followed by a small embarrassment – it all can add up to the point where a woman says, "I'll do anything. I'll be thin at any cost."

It has been seventeen years since my father's death, but I find that he is never far from my thoughts. I think of those early comments he made about my weight and I sigh. The words of a father are *so* critical for the self-esteem of a young girl. But I forgive him and I miss him terribly. And every Christmas Eve at the candlelight service I stand and hold my candle and choke out the words to Silent Night, Kleenex in hand, dabbing my eyes as if his death were yesterday. Ronia has said to me, "Invite him into your dreams and he will come and visit you." But as of yet, he has not made an appearance with any sort of obvious message.

My mother and my sister continue to be the primary members of my inner circle. They have walked with me every step of the way -- through West Point, my marriage, my father's death, my divorce and the fight to overcome my eating disorder. I often say to them, "We've walked a long road together" and they agree.

We have new players in our lives now. Much to our surprise, after twelve years alone, my mother remarried in 2006 to a man we like and admire. He is intelligent and classy, just like my father, but brings new qualities of his own. He fills the role of grandfather to my nieces and nephew and occasionally, for me, he fills in for my dad. My mother and her husband live eight miles away from me in a cottage that has been in our family for five generations.

My sister lives eight miles in the opposite direction. Her husband is a fireman – a good guy. They have two beautiful daughters and a wonderful little boy. My nieces are the next two girls in a "long line of strong women." And already, during a recent drive into New York, the eldest looked at me and said, "It's a wonderful city." I smiled at her and nodded.

My family, like any other, has its highs and lows. But we all work at it. We make an effort to stay connected. There is healthy debate and mutual respect.

And now my bulimia is a part of our family history.

I wish that I could say that post-treatment, I am whole and healthy-minded and never lament my shape and size. But I still think about my weight all the time. I still wish I were thinner. I lament the clothes I no longer fit into. But would I go back to 127 pounds and purging four times a day?

Not in a million years.

Recently, while heading out on a business trip, I caught a glimpse of myself in one of the big windows at Kennedy Airport.

I looked sharp. I looked like "her."

I was ten years old the first time my family flew to Missouri to see Aunt Birdie and right there in the terminal I had seen "the woman." She was beautifully dressed and striding toward us with an air of confidence and sophistication. She wore a navy blue suit with a white blouse and carried a briefcase in her hand. Her nails were done and her hair was in a neat chignon in the back of her head. This was a woman who was in *charge* of something. She was a leader. I thought to myself, *I want to be her.*

And now I am.

EPILOGUE

N ew Cadet, step up to my line," said the cadet in the red sash.

"Yes Sir," I popped off in reply.

I stepped up to the red line on the concrete and assumed the position of attention. I was participating in "Cadet for a Day," in which civilians volunteer to play the part of the incoming fourth class so that the cadre can practice their lines and the stages of the day so that they are well prepared for R Day. To participate in the Beast practice required only a phone call. I was in civilian clothes and no one was the wiser that once I had stood where they now did, dressed in white over grey.

Different from my R Day, the station with the "cadet in the red sash" now took place in one of the sallyports. But the location didn't matter. The experience was the same. It all came rushing back – me as a plebe getting my ass handed to me for some infraction, me as a cadet pinging through the barracks, doing pushups, falling in love with my squad leader.

As I walked from checkpoint to checkpoint, so much was unchanged. Voices of upper class cadets filled the Area. I was given a moment to use the latrine and I took a moment to glance in the room of one of the upperclassmen. His bed was pushed against the wall, neatly made up with USMA grey blanket, the white sheet folded a clipboard's width at the top. His shoes were lined up in a row next to his combat boots under the bed. It was my room, just twenty years later.

The barracks smelled the same.

The cadets looked the same.

But I wasn't the same.

I had traveled a long road, had nearly lost my life to my bulimia, only to rebuild it. My addiction and recovery made West Point seem a distant accomplishment.

The cadre took a moment to regroup for the next round of practice and the "new cadets" were given a reprieve for a few minutes. I used the break to ask the question I was dying to ask.

"I was wondering," I said to one of the women, "How life is now as a female cadet. Are you having a good experience? Do you feel accepted?"

"Yes," she smiled in reply, "for the most part it's fine. There are always the parts that are miserable, but I think they're miserable for everybody."

I nodded and pressed on.

"When I was here," I continued, "there was tremendous pressure to be thin. Do you feel that pressure too?"

"Not really," she replied, considering the answer, "I think most cadets just accept that the female cadets may not make weight on the scale and have to be taped. But most people recognize that we're just built differently."

"That's wonderful to hear," I nodded, hoping it was true.

She smiled in reply and went on to her next task.

"New Cadet!" the shout came.

"Yes Sir," I popped off automatically.

It was late afternoon. Most of the cadre were wrapping up.

But the day was far from over for me. I was on my way to the airport to fly to Europe on business. Without hesitation I turned my wrist and looked at the time.

"New Cadet, you can't just fall out!" the firstie barked at me, "Do you think you can just look at your watch whenever you please!?"

I looked at the Area where I had stood so long ago and then at him.

"Yes, Cadet, I certainly can," I replied with a grin, "I did this part of my life already. It's been twenty years since I stood in this spot. But now I've got a plane to catch."

I reached out and shook the hand of the surprised firstie in front of me.

"I wish you the best of luck on R Day. Knock 'em dead!"

I turned to go and walked out of Central Area and down the sidewalk to the other side of the Plain.

Then, getting into my car, I put West Point in the rear view mirror.

CPSIA information can be obtained at www.ICGtesting.com
Printed in the USA
BVOW071821061211

277739BV00004B/5/P